Shad Helmstetter,Ph.D.

American Victory

The Real Story of
Today's Amway

Chapel
&
Croft
Publishing

Other books by Shad Helmstetter:

Network Of Champions

What To Say When You Talk To Your Self

The Self-Talk Solution

Choices

Predictive Parenting—
   What To Say When You Talk To Your Kids

Finding The Fountain Of Youth Inside Yourself

Self-Talk For Weight-Loss

You Can Excel In Times Of Change

AMERICAN VICTORY

Helmstetter, Shad
    American Victory

ISBN 0-9645171-6-7

Printed in USA

10 9 8 7 6 5 4 3

To the Distributors

This book is dedicated with belief, encouragement, and respect, to Amway Distributors everywhere. You're making a difference. This book is for you.

Contents

Shad Helmstetter, Ph.D.

American Victory

Part I
In Pursuit Of A Dream

*"You can choose
to work for yourself.*

*You can choose to become
financially independent.*

*You can choose to have freedom
for the rest of your life.*

And you can choose to succeed."

Chapter One
Choosing To Succeed

T his book is about choosing to succeed. It's a book about the Amway business, but more importantly, it's about you, your goals, your family, your career, and your success.

This is the second book I've written about "the business." My first book, "*Network Of Champions*," was written with a very specific objective in mind: to *recognize*, to *teach*, to *motivate*, and to *inspire* you. This second book for you, after more research into your organization, is written with those same important goals in mind:

To *recognize* you and acknowledge the important job you're doing as an Amway Distributor.

To *teach* you the best of what I've learned in my career in motivational behavior.

To *motivate* you to follow both your head and your heart, and make the decision to build your business.

And to *inspire* you to dream—and to make your dreams come true.

A PRACTICAL, DOWN-TO-EARTH, COMMON SENSE APPROACH TO BEING SUCCESSFUL

I've never been one to believe in pipe-dreams. If it isn't practical, if it doesn't work, I don't want any part of it.

At the same time, I've long believed that most people sell themselves short. They don't get the most out of their lives. They settle for too little, and instead of their lives being exceptional, their lives are ordinary, and unremarkable, and unfulfilled.

In this book you'll find a practical, down-to-earth, common sense approach to being successful.

Throughout my professional career of writing, and speaking to audiences about the best ways to be successful in life, I've always looked for that one best way to get the job done. "What would I tell my own friend to do, if he were to ask me what he should do with the rest of his life?"

I hope what you read in the pages that follow will let you know you are that friend.

NO MATTER WHERE YOU ARE IN THE BUSINESS TODAY

This book is written for four different kinds of people—all of whom have the same potential in front of them.

It is written for:

1. People who are *new to the business,*

2. People who are *experienced Amway Distributors,*

3. People who *have been in the business for some time but haven't yet committed to making it work,* and

4. People who are *considering becoming a distributor,* but who aren't yet in the business.

Whichever of these categories you may fit into, this book is written for you.

1. If you're new to the Amway business.

If you're new to the business—*you made the right choice.* Go ahead and feel good about it.

If you work at it, and build your Amway business, I wish I could adequately tell you what you have in store for you.

The complete picture of a future with Amway deserves more than a motivational talk or a two-hour presentation, or even a few pages in a book. What you're dealing with here is an idea and a plan and a career that could well change the rest of your life.

If you're new to the business, I can only suggest that you take what you read here as seriously as you've ever taken any one-on-one conversation in your life. Throughout this book it will be *me* talking to *you*—just like we were sitting together in your living room or in mine.

What I share with you in the following pages could not be more heartfelt or sincere if I were talking to my own sons or nephews or nieces. My goal is for them to succeed. My goal is for *you* to succeed.

If you're new to the Amway business, *you should feel good about your choice.* This book is about being on the right track—and how to do even better on that track. If you're already in the business, and working at being a success, you made the right choice. *You are definitely in the right place.*

2. If you're already experienced in the Amway business.

If you've been in the business for some time, no matter how well you've done up to now, it's time for you to *renew.*

This book is about a *re*commitment. It's a what-to-do and how-to-do-it book for creating a new contract with success.

If you want to do it—if you *really* want to do it—this book will help you make that commitment.

Also, while you move up to your next level in the business, it's a good idea to bring your own downline along with you. What you read in the following pages is written to help you, and it's written to help them.

3. If you've been in the business for some time, but haven't yet committed to making it work.

If you haven't done it yet, *regroup and revitalize.* This book is also written for those people who have worked hard at their business, or at least now and then, but it just hasn't worked out for them the way they thought it should.

In the chapters that follow, you'll find some of the tools that will help you take that next important step—the step toward real commitment to your future.

If everyone who has been in the business for five, or ten, or even fifteen years would make the decision, *this year*, right now, *to make the business work,* the Amway business in general—and yours—would double overnight. If you were one of those distributors who decided to make that change, not only would the breadth and scope of your Amway business change . . . so would your *life*.

If you read carefully, and put into practice what you find, this book will help you make that change.

4. *If you're considering becoming an Amway Distributor and building a business for yourself.*

If, right now, you and I could just sit and talk together for an hour or two, and if you were considering the decision whether or not to become an Amway Distributor, I would tell you some things that would probably surprise you. I'm certain that what I would tell you would be important to you and to your future.

I've done my best to include my personal message to you in the pages of this book. I hope you get the message.

NO MATTER WHERE YOU ARE, THIS IS FOR YOU

If you're new to the business, you made the right choice—you're in the right place.

If you're experienced in the business—it's time to *renew*.

If you've been in the business for some time, but haven't done it yet—it's time to *regroup and revitalize*.

If you're considering the business—it's time to get started. You have probably found the best means you'll ever find to take control of your own life.

For everyone reading this book, no matter what level you're at now, it's my objective that by the end of this book you'll have a better, clearer idea of where you're going with your life—and how building your Amway business can help you get there.

Let me get right to the point: Amway works. The idea of Amway works. The concept of free enterprise works. Building an independent Amway business works. Creating better lives by helping other people build their own Amway businesses works.

The question of whether Amway works is no longer a question that is posed by informed people. If you want to build a future—a *successful* future—that you control, there may be no better thing you can do today than to be a part of the Amway Distributor organization.

*"Your Amway business gives you
the opportunity to succeed
in every important area
of your life.*

*This business builds your faith,
your family, your friendships,
your freedom,
and your future."*

Chapter Two

A Dream You Can Believe In

Thereis a story that needs to be told. It's a story the whole world ought to hear. (And the way things are going, the world *will* hear it.)

It's a story so significant to you and your business that I decided to follow up on the story personally, get all the facts, and make certain that what I suspected was true.

To research this story, my wife Elise and I traveled to other cities in the U.S., and even to other countries. We spent hours interviewing the people who were at the heart of the story. And when we were finished, I couldn't help but wonder how many Amway Distributors today understand what this story really means.

I'd like to briefly tell you the story as *I* see it—from my own outside perspective.

To begin with, let me make a small disclaimer. If you've read any of my previous books, you may know that I never spotlight any one person. I don't write about success by relating stories about sports figures or other famous people.

I've always felt those stories were usually better written by someone else. During the course of writing eight previous books in the field of personal growth, I chose to focus on specific techniques instead of specific people. Besides, the minute you write about someone special, you leave out all the other people who are equally special. That, of course, is not my intention.

But in this book, for the first time ever, and for good reasons, I've decided to mention some people by name. It doesn't mean there aren't other special people out there—but for you to understand the importance of this story, you have to know the people who made this story happen.

THE TRUTH ABOUT AMWAY, AND
THE THREE GENERATIONS

If you've been in the business any time at all, you've already learned that Amway is now a *three*-generation business. That is, someone who became an Amway Distributor, and went Direct, had a son who started his own Amway business and went Direct, and *that* son had a son who started *his* own Amway business and went Direct.

The significance of that is astounding. I suspect you're familiar with that scenario of success in the business, but I've looked deeper into the story. I'd like you to know what it *really* means—especially for you, and your *own* Amway business.

The family who first earned the distinction of having three generations of Directs in the business was, of course, the Victor family. So that you understand the significance of what they did, here's an overview of what took place.

REMEMBER THIS STORY, SO YOU CAN TELL IT TO YOUR KIDS—AND TO YOUR GRANDCHILDREN

Joe and Helyne Victor were one of the original "founding families" of Amway Distributors, before the business was even called Amway. In the early years of the business, there were distributors in only two states—Michigan and Ohio—and they only had one product to sell.

It was clear to these pioneers that the *concept* of the business was even more important than any one product, so they got together and decided to build a long-term business that was based on *principles*, rather than on products alone. The products would have to be good, of course—the best—but the business itself would have to be based on principles.

At those early meetings, Joe Victor and the other distributors were meeting in the Victor living room and having discussions that probably sounded more like the founding fathers of our country discussing the Declaration of Independence, than a group of people creating a new approach to business.

What those pioneers decided to do was to build the future

of their young business based on personal integrity, values, faith in God, the importance of the family, the importance of people helping people, and building a business that would have an unlimited future.

FIVE PRINCIPLES THAT BUILT A BUSINESS AND CHANGED THE WORLD

They chose to lay out five principles they felt strongly about, and base the business on those principles.

First, the business they were about to build would have to be *Universal*—that is, it would be a business for people from all walks of life.

Second, the business would be based on *Repeat* business—that is, it would be a business that would establish an ongoing, positive relationship with its customers. This would not be a one-time sale or purchase. The new business, and the distributors who built this business, would have to be there, counted on, year after year.

Third, the business should be set up to be *Unlimited*. That's an incredible concept for a new business. No limits. No limits in thinking. No limits in growth. No limits in accepting new technology. No limits in the potential of people. *No limits.*

Fourth, the pioneers decided that this business should not be a business that was dependent on the *Economy*. The founding distributors had all lived through the Depression, and they recognized the necessity of building a business that did not

13

depend on the ups and downs of the stock market or the mood swings of the buying public.

And fifth, the first distributors set forth that each distributor that followed them would have the opportunity to own and operate his own business—to enjoy the benefits and the unlimited opportunities available to them from something called *Free Enterprise.*

THE *FIRST* GENERATION OF AMWAY DISTRIBUTORS CREATED THE *SECOND* GENERATION

While those founding pioneers of Amway Distributors were sitting and talking in Joe Victor's living room, there was a kid, Joe's son, who would bring the coffee into the meeting room. His biggest goal at the time was to be able to bring the coffee in without spilling it.

Young Jody Victor considered his dad his greatest hero. He got to listen in. He got to be there. And it would change the course of his life.

Young Jody wasn't spending his youth arguing over who got to watch what on television. He was watching the creation of a new Declaration of Independence. He was listening. And he was learning.

In time, after enrolling in college, studying accounting, and then entering law school, the picture of *those* men, the first-hand knowledge of *that* business, the understanding of *those* principles, all came together. And still-young Jody Victor

14

made a decision that would change his life—and the lives of countless others—forever.

He spent his own money, and bought a Starter Kit. He became an independent Amway Distributor, and he decided to build his own business.

Years earlier, Joe Victor had become a Direct Distributor, and then, step-by-step, reached each next level of success in the business.

Then Jody Victor became a Direct Distributor, and, in time, he and his wife Kathy began their own path toward becoming Crown Ambassadors.

When I did my research, I found it interesting to note that no one *expected* Jody Victor to automatically become a distributor and build his own Amway business. His father didn't push him, or expect him to do it. Joe had set the example. He had ordained a path to the future. He had cast the mold, and it was a very good one.

THE *THIRD* GENERATION ENTERS THE STAGE

Then the next extraordinary step took place: Jody's son Steve, and Steve's wife Marcia, became Direct Distributors after starting their own Amway business.

To put that into perspective, well over a quarter of a century after Joe Victor helped lay out the principles that would end up guiding every distributor who is now building an Amway business, Joe Victor's *grandson* went Direct in the same business.

When I learned this, the first thing I wanted to do was interview Steve. I had some questions I wanted to ask him. My wife Elise and I had had the opportunity to meet and get to know—and interview—Jody and Kathy Victor at length. Jody himself had even said, "If you want to know me, you ought to interview my kids."

He was right. If you want to know the man, or the woman, talk to their kids. So I did.

When I interviewed Steve, after he and Marcia had gone Direct, I asked him whether it had been easier for him than it would be for other distributors. His answer was that it was probably harder. After all, when he started in the business—for himself—he had to go it alone. All of his family and friends had already been shown the plan.

He could have given up in discouragement. But as Steve told me, "I soon figured out there's a whole world out there. I just have to work the plan like everybody else."

THE REASON WHY IT WORKED

There's an important reason for spotlighting this one family here, and sharing their story with you.

Joe Victor, hugely successful in the business, did not push or expect his son to do the same. He left the choice up to his son.

Later, Jody Victor, hugely successful in the business, did not push or expect any of his children to do the same. He left the choice up to them.

16

When I interviewed Steve Victor, I asked him about his goals. He very quickly listed several clearly defined goals for me. One of them was that he would be able to bring a *fourth*-generation distributor into the business.

Will Steve and Marcia, as they make their way toward Diamondhood, and then on to Crown Ambassadors themselves, try to persuade their own son or daughter to enter the business?

My guess is they'll let their kids make that decision for themselves. Just as Jody and Kathy did. Just as Joe and Helyne did. But if I had to guess, I would bet on most Amway kids everywhere, somewhere down the line, making the choice to get a Starter Kit for themselves, making the choice to build the business, and making the choice to build a life.

That's what Amway does. That's why Amway works.

IT'S TIME TO WRITE YOUR OWN STORY
FOR YOURSELF

There is a profound significance to that story.

That story, if you think about it, proves the most important point you could ever make about this business. The first Victor, Joe, made the decision to build a quality business. No one forced him to make that decision. Then, young son Jody watched his parents build a business based on values, and he too, *on his own*, decided to start and build an Amway business. Then young son Steve watched Jody and Kathy

17

build a value-based business, and once again, he took responsibility for himself, and decided to build an Amway business. And make it work.

Joe Victor didn't have to build his business, but he did. Jody Victor didn't have to build *his* own Amway business, but he did. And with all that success, and with all that prosperity (his parents and his grandparents were already upper-level Diamonds in the business), Steve Victor most certainly did not have to build *his* own Amway business for himself. But he did.

Why did they do that?

Each of them knew the whole story. Each of them knew the goods and the bads, the possibilities and the difficulties. Each of them is intelligent, thinks for himself, and takes responsibility for his own actions. And each of them, on his own, made the choice to be in the business.

Why?

THEY DID IT BECAUSE THE BUSINESS WORKS— AND THE BUSINESS CAN WORK FOR YOU

I've related the Victor story to you here because it's important to know what people *who know,* do about the business.

I fully expect to be there when the *fourth*-generation Victor walks across the stage and receives his or her recognition for going Direct in the business. That would be the *great*-grandson or great-granddaughter of the first Victors in the business. I've met the Victors. I suspect that will happen.

Their story is second only to the story you now have the opportunity to write for yourself. What will *you* do in the business? How many of *your* descendants will choose to do the same?

A BUSINESS BASED ON VALUES

To me, the story of the three generations of Victors says two very important things:

First, it proves beyond any doubt, any question, that the business works. Not just for some people, but for everyone. The kids in that story didn't have it better than you; they had to follow the same road you do.

What they had, that some people don't, was the *belief.* They had seen it work. If they hadn't, they wouldn't have chosen *on their own* to be in it. They believed in it. *So can you.*

And second, it proves there's more to the Amway business than products and points. Reaching your next level is important, without a doubt.

But I suspect those second and third generation Amway Distributors knew something else about the business. It may have been the *other* reasons that made them decide to join the team.

Perhaps it was because they saw their parents living a life of independence and freedom—the kind of life most people talk about, but few people ever live.

Perhaps it was because they saw what happens when you live your life—and manage your business—based on values: integrity, belief in others, personal faith, honest work, and personal responsibility. Perhaps they saw those values in action—and saw them work.

Or maybe it was just because they were smart enough to figure out that no one, anywhere, ever, has built a business quite like the Amway business. Built on principles, built on the exceptional foundation of people helping people to succeed, built on values, and *built to last*.

When Jody Victor says, *"I watched my parents in pursuit of a dream . . ."* he knows his own son Steve can, and does, say exactly the same thing. The third generation proves that same dream is still alive and well today. That's a dream you can believe in—and make it come true for you.

WHAT *THEY* CAN DO—*YOU* CAN DO

My hat is off to the Victors. I have great respect for them, and I have great respect for the other leaders of your business who, though I have not mentioned them here by name, have proved the greatness of their spirit, the endurance of their ideals, and the quality of their character.

They have built *for you* the bedrock of a business, and the chance for a future, that may never be equaled.

WHAT THIS MEANS TO YOU RIGHT NOW

If you're not yet in the business, may I offer this suggestion from a researcher who has studied this business thoroughly:

It's time to join. It's time to start. It's time to build your future for yourself. In my research I've studied the best of them. There are a lot of pretenders. But there's nothing that comes close to the real thing. The real thing is Amway.

If you *are* in the business right now, dig in, get serious, build it, and make it big. There's nothing to stop you from doing that but you.

As a major business today, and as an even bigger business of the future, there's no doubt that Amway is, and will be, *incredibly successful*. You deserve to be a part of that success, and you deserve to make it work for you.

The rest of this book will show you how.

Part II
Amway Distributor University

*"Choose to improve your life
in every way you can.*

*Make the decision to learn
something new
every day.*

*Never let a day go by
without getting better."*

Chapter Three
Welcome To ADU

If you want to make your future work, in anything you're going to do, you've got to go to school. Fortunately, as an Amway Distributor, you're already enrolled; if you're in the business, you're already a student in the most incredible "school" you'll ever attend.

But in this school there aren't any entrance exams; you qualify by wanting to make life better for you and for others. Most of the tuition will be paid for with the time you put in. There will be some course materials you'll need—in this school they're called tools—and you'll have to do some independent study.

You'll have the most highly-skilled teachers, the best encouragement, and a clear curriculum to follow. The grades will be 100% fair—your grade will be based entirely on how much effort you put into your studies.

Your campus will be your business, and your classroom will be your life.

Now, shall we make sure you're properly enrolled? And while we're at it, why don't we go ahead and schedule your graduation?

WELCOME TO ADU—
AMWAY DISTRIBUTOR UNIVERSITY

Amway doesn't officially call their training program a university—ADU is my name for it—but make no mistake: that's what it is, and it's one of the best.

If there were a college named Amway Distributor University, and its economic output and leadership training program were exactly what Amway's are today, there would be a waiting list so long no one would ever be able to get in!

Pretend for a moment that ADU was to exist as an actual university—with tree-lined campuses, ivy-covered buildings, and an impressive roster of distinguished faculty members.

Let's say that ADU, this Amway University, has a curriculum whose purpose it is "to prepare its students to be successful in business, or to create lasting benefits among people and cultures throughout the world."

That would be a university not unlike many that grace our cities and states today.

Now let's look at what the "invisible" school, the Amway Distributor University, has accomplished. Let's look at its total output in teaching personal growth, free enterprise, and the worldwide social and economic growth created by its students.

25

COMPARE YOUR SCHOOL—
AMWAY DISTRIBUTOR UNIVERSITY—
TO ALL THE OTHERS

A school is an institution that's supposed to prepare you to succeed in life. So let's compare Amway's output and productivity with other schools, to see how ADU stacks up. Choose whichever college or university you like.

Amway Distributor University has an impressive list of accomplishments, perhaps unequaled by any other school, anywhere.

First let's look at teaching people how to be successful in business.

You could try to count the hundred-thousandaires and even millionaires, I suppose. If there's another business school that singlehandedly creates more entrepreneurial successes, I don't know of it.

Great wealth, of course, isn't even the point. It's good to create wealth, and it's essential to build financial independence if you want to have real freedom in your life.

In that role, ADU can be proud of its accomplishments. But even more important, Amway is teaching free enterprise, the economic system that *creates* financial independence in the first place. When it comes to teaching the solid basics of free enterprise, I doubt any other school can get close to ADU.

Let's not stop there. Of the universities surrounding us today that teach something called "social economics," how many of *their* graduates are literally changing the face of business and creating the growth of free enterprise *around the world?*

How many major university graduate students can attract thousands of new independent business owners to a business conference in Brazil, or thousands more in Poland, as an example?

Or what about the third-world countries with their under-nourished minds, starving for knowledge, and their impoverished spirits crying out for freedom? These people, with their once-forgotten potential, are not going to be brought to life with a government food-stamp program, or bureaucrats who line up to keep them in line. Not if graduate students of ADU are there. And, fortunately, graduates of Amway University *are* there.

GUESS WHO'S CHANGING THE WORLD FOR THE BETTER, RIGHT WHERE YOU LIVE?

What school, university, or institution is actually making a difference for the better where you live and work right now?

Who is busy changing the business climate and making positive changes in your own city, or in the state you live in? The very nature of business in your own country and in your hometown is changing.

People are learning what independence and freedom feel like—and they like what they're finding. People are learning they like to be their own boss, set their own hours, follow their own goal plans, take responsibility for their own futures, and actually get to enjoy the rewards they create.

I don't have to tell you which university stands at the forefront of one of the most important shifts in product distribution and personal business growth this country has ever seen. The organization responsible for leading the trend that is right now changing the way this country does business, is Amway.

Obviously, then, the university responsible for training the leaders of this positive business revolution must be the invisible one. ADU.

THE MOST IMPORTANT EDUCATION OF ALL

The most important part of the story isn't even about business itself. It's the part Amway plays in inspiring people and building their attitudes about the most essential elements of their lives.

The values that ADU builds so well are at the heart of everything that works right about this country—and every *other* country.

And ADU doesn't even have to measure itself against other schools to see how well it shapes up. The truth is: *There are no other schools in the public sector that teach the values Amway teaches.*

Even your association with Amway affects your most important attitudes about yourself and your life: your self-esteem, how you feel about personal growth, your sense of honesty and integrity, your marriage, the importance of your family, your goals, the value of good honest hard work, the depth of your faith, and your willingness to wait for the reward.

I've been studying the formulas and ingredients for successful living for many years. If there's a better grounding than your association with Amway, for the creation of true success in your life, I haven't found it.

THE ADU LEADERSHIP TRAINING
PROGRAM

The Amway Distributor organization doesn't call it this, but without a doubt they have the most advanced "Leadership Training Program" you will find.

Have you ever wondered how Diamonds learn how to be Diamonds? How to talk in front of audiences, what to say, what to wear, how to act, when to be where, or what to do next?

How do Emeralds know how to be Emeralds—with the poise and self-confidence that so many Emeralds are able to exhibit so naturally? How does each person, at each level, get the knowledge he or she needs to excel at that level? How do ascending Amway Distributors, at every step of the upward way, know how to manage, counsel, maintain, and support the distributors around them?

To begin with, let's get rid of the myth that suggests that Diamonds start out special or different—that they're born that way. We may all be born to be Diamonds—to excel—but no one gets there by accident.

DIAMONDS, LIKE CHAMPIONS,
ARE MADE—NOT BORN

Diamonds and other Amway leaders were born in the same hospitals as you and I were. Same kinds of parents. Same prospects. Same schools. Same friends. Same problems. Same chances. Same everything.

So how, then, did they become leaders?

Was it that they were lucky? Were they selected in some special way? Did someone on high single them out and change the odds in their favor?

The answer is an important one: Amway leaders became the leaders they are today because they got sponsored, became distributors, followed the plan, worked hard, *and were trained for leadership*.

They were taught. They were *prepared* for success in advance.

It's comforting to know that when you see a Diamond on the stage, bright, confident and glowing, that that same Diamond was once sitting in your chair watching some other Diamond on that stage. The team at the top all started out at the bottom. And they reached their levels by being *trained* to reach their levels.

Within the Amway organization, you are *prepared* for any level of "management" you're about to reach.

Few other businesses have been able to prepare their people so well. What most businesses do is train people only for the most immediate job in front of them. They don't try to build broad, lifetime skills.

People these days don't stay with one company long

enough for that kind of training. The average company knows that if they give someone too much training, they're just training someone they'll lose anyhow.

So how is it that Amway solved this problem, and turned it into one of their greatest assets? It all starts with the Amway organization's basic belief in distributors—and therefore leaders—as *people*.

ADU TEACHES LEADERSHIP THAT IS BASED ON THE PERSONAL GROWTH AND DEVELOPMENT OF THE *INDIVIDUAL*

The heart of the Amway Leadership Training Program is to *recognize the true potential of you, as an individual—and bring that promise to life.*

That means that when any Amway Distributor at the Leadership level talks to you, he doesn't see an average person who may or may not amount to anything; instead, he sees *you*, a real person, with every attribute you have right now (strength, need, potential, etc.) ready to be nurtured, guided, taught, and stayed with—to the limits of your potential.

As any of them will tell you, most Amway leaders don't believe there *are* any practical limits to your potential.

TEACHERS AND TRAINERS WHO BELIEVE IN *YOU*

31

That isn't to say your leaders aren't realistic, or practical. They tend to be very realistic. That's part of their training. But they know that most of your limitations are imagined. And they understand that you have more potential than most *other* people would ever recognize. They also know you have more potential than *you* probably recognize.

It's almost as though the Amway Leadership Training Program *begins* exactly where the average business training program *stops*.

The average business training program attempts to train you for a job; the Amway Leadership Training trains you for a *life*.

The reason that no other business trains like Amway is because few other businesses believe in you, the individual, like Amway does. How could a company help you develop your full potential if they don't take the time to *understand* your potential in the first place?

Amway leaders don't only see your potential; they also understand the *obstacles* you have that might get in your way. They know you're human. They're still human. They came from the same place you did. They had just as much to learn, just as much to get past, just as much disbelief, and just as many flaws that needed fixing.

When you listen to their stories of their growth in the business, it's very clear: These leaders are real people who *learned* how to overcome their imperfections, stop thinking average, get past the bad, and start building the good.

The key word here is *learned*.

Each of them attended ADU, and they had teachers of their own—the dedicated, professional, highly trained leaders who came before them.

Now those same students, the ones who learned how to grow, are *themselves* dedicated, professional, highly trained, and ready to share. Now *they* are leaders—and they're ready to help *you*.

AT THE *HEART* OF THE TEACHING— ## ARE TEACHERS WITH *HEART*

You may, as an Amway Distributor, see your upline as "the people above you," or as the people who just happen to be at higher levels than you are at today.

But I'd suggest a different perspective. Begin to see your upline as your *teachers*, in the most important school you'll ever attend. None of them *just happens* to be there. The true teachers among your upline are where they are because they've already been where you're about to go.

I've spent many hours with your leaders—the men and women who are your teachers. During the past few years I've had many long conversations with them—about the business, about their lives, about their beliefs, about their dreams.

What do you suppose they talk about most? The products? The business profits? The company policies? Their own hard work?

None of those. They talk about *you*.

They talk about their commitment to you. They talk about believing in you and refusing to give up. I've observed these leaders closely as they share the thoughts that are closest to their hearts and always on their minds. I have so often seen the look in their eyes, a very personal belief, when they discuss your great road ahead, and the future that's in front of you.

That look I see is their caring, hoping that you, too, see the same life and future in front of you that *they* see in front of you.

TRUE TEACHING IS EDUCATING, MOTIVATING, ENCOURAGING, AND SHARING

Your strongest leaders are often, in their private moments, like very fine parents—the kind that all of us would like to be. They talk as fondly about *you* as they talk about their children, hoping for the best for you, and praying they are doing everything they can to help you attain it.

As my wife Elise and I have traveled across the U.S. and to other countries, attending functions and conferences, speaking to the distributors and meeting and getting to know all of those leaders—in city after city, leader after leader, we have always found the same thing: these are leaders who spend nearly all of their waking time teaching, building, encouraging—and *all* of their time caring.

What other business managers do that? How many companies do you know whose *entire management teams* spend most all of their time teaching—and *all* of their time caring about the people they work with?

It's clear that in the recipe for "*what makes Amway work so well,*" a key combination of ingredients is *an absolute belief in you as a person*, and a training program that, if you *listen, practice,* and *learn*, will take you as far as you want to go, no matter how far that is.

AN "ALMA MATER"—AND A *FUTURE*— YOU CAN BE PROUD OF

I encourage you to become a good student of your remarkable Amway Distributor University—the best student you can possibly be.

Take your training and all of the teaching seriously. The teaching you receive is generously given; be just as generous in your desire to *listen*, to *practice*, to *learn*, and to *improve yourself.*

Look for the lessons. Get an *education* from the Amway University. Use the tools. Study hard. Decide to excel. And make good grades.

I've met the graduate students of ADU. I like them. They are champions. You're fortunate that these winners have now become your teachers.

To my observation, your school—ADU—in the form of the Amway Distributor organization, *does* exist—and if you're in the business, you're already enrolled.

Now that you're in school, *if you work at it*, you'll join the ranks of some of the most all-around successful people that are alive today. They are the alumni of ADU.

Every one of them is pulling for you. With their teaching and guidance, *if you want to succeed, you can.*

YOUR PERSONAL ADU COURSE LIST

It would be almost impossible to list every subject area you can learn as a student of ADU, but the following list includes many of them.

Each of the "courses" on the list can be studied, worked on, or practiced.

I recommend that you make your own separate list of which courses you need to take, in the areas you need to work on.

When you make your list, don't overload yourself with courses. Start with selecting the three or four areas you'd like to work on first. Review your list frequently, and add other courses to your curriculum when you're ready.

Here are some of the things you can learn at ADU:

ADU COURSE LIST

☐ Goal Setting
☐ Dream Building
☐ Time Management
☐ Attitude Building
☐ Self-Motivation
☐ Prospecting
☐ Showing The Plan
☐ Reading Habits
☐ Using Tools
☐ Believing In The Business
☐ Attending Seminars And Functions
☐ Financial Planning

☐ Work Habits
☐ Family Involvement
☐ Delayed Gratification
☐ Speaking And Presenting
☐ Overcoming Objections
☐ Dealing With Negatives
☐ Building Self-Esteem
☐ (Other personal or business areas you need to work on)
☐ _____
☐ _____
☐ _____

Talk your personal course list over with your spouse. Show your list to your counselor (usually your sponsors, or your upline mentors). Just as when you enroll in school, your mentors will give you guidance, suggest the right tools, and help you set and follow a schedule.

Learn from your upline, use the tools, listen to the tapes, study the videos, attend the seminars and functions, practice what you learn, and make the choice to graduate at the top of the class.

"Graduation exercises" are each pin level you achieve. Go ahead and schedule each of your pin levels, and set actual dates. And don't forget to give yourself a "graduation present" when you reach each level. Scheduling your rewards is just as important as planning your success.

Attend Amway Distributor University. Work hard, study hard, practice what you learn, and make something out of yourself.

If you do that, I have no doubt you'll do well in the rest of your life. ADU is an incredible school. And you'll get an education you will get nowhere else.

At Amway Distributor University, you:

Learn to learn.
Learn to grow.
Learn to succeed.

That *is*, after all, *what we go to school for in the first place.*

"When it comes to building
your Amway business,
tools are not an option—
tools are essential.

Use the tools,
and build your business."

Chapter Four
The Six Rules Of Tools

One of the most important aspects of Amway Distributor University is the "study materials"—otherwise known as *tools*. For the past several years, I've observed the development and use of Amway tools; I've watched people use them, watched the results, and assessed their improvement. I've also compared your tools and materials to the other "training aids" that are available elsewhere.

I've come to some clear conclusions about your tools. I've outlined my observations in the form of six *"Rules of Tools"* that sum up what you should know about the business tools available to you through your organization.

TOOL RULE #1:
If you want to succeed in the business, tools are not an option—they are *essential*.

Your upline doesn't require you to use the tools, of course. You don't have to take advantage of the tools to be a distributor, or to be in the business.

I'm speaking from a strictly outside point of view that makes a lot of sense. You don't *have* to use tools, true. But on the other hand, intelligent people *look* for things that will help them improve, instead of trying to get by with as little as possible.

Some distributors put off using the tools for any number of reasons—none of them good ones. Their reasons are actually nothing more than excuses: "I don't have the time." "I can't afford them." "I don't need the tools." "I'll make my own." "We're going to start using them (later) . . ."

HOW MUCH DO YOU *KNOW*?—AND WHAT *ACTION* DO YOU TAKE?

There are only two basic ingredients in *any* success. There is *Knowledge* and there is *Action*.

That's it. Put what you *know* together with what you *do*, and that will determine whether you make it or not. If you don't *know* enough, you won't make it. If you don't *do* enough, or do the right thing, you won't make it. But if you put the right knowledge together with the right action, you get a success formula that works.

YOU ARE WHAT YOU KNOW

First let's take your knowledge.

How much do you know? That is, when it comes to the business, how much do you *really* know? How much actual experience do you have being highly successful in this business?

If you have not yet been in the business for many years, and been very successful during that time, then you need *knowledge*. You need to learn what the most successful, most experienced experts in the business have learned.

The truth is: *tools are borrowed experience.*

If you want to make it in the business, if you don't yet have the successful experience yourself, then you have to borrow it from someone else until you can get more of your own.

WHERE CAN YOU GO TO LEARN WHAT YOU NEED TO KNOW?

Imagine walking up to the president of any large successful corporation and saying, *"Excuse me, would you loan me all of your experience? Would you mind spending hours and hours teaching me and training me and telling me all of your secrets so I can be successful just like you?"* He would probably look at you strangely, shake his head, and walk away—or call security to escort you out.

Meanwhile, your Amway leaders are lining up to help you. And they're a whole lot bigger and more successful than most of those company presidents will ever be. (Maybe *your leaders* know something other business leaders *don't*.)

Your own Amway Diamonds and your other leaders are among the most successful business people in the world. And yet *they're* saying to you, *"I'll tell you what. We'll spend hours and hours teaching you and training you. We'll loan you all of our experience. We'll teach you everything we have learned; we'll share all of our secrets of success with you. And meanwhile we'll encourage you, and stay with you, and do everything we can to help you."*

All they ask is that you be willing to listen carefully, and have a sincere desire to *learn* and *practice* what they're sharing with you. Learn and practice; *knowledge and action*—the two key parts of success. *The tools give you the knowledge.* Without it, you cannot succeed.

TOOL RULE #2:
Use the tools every day. Not now and then. *Every day*.

The distributors who excel most naturally are always the distributors who have made a habit of using tools. They read something from a recommended book during some time each day. They listen to tapes as a way of life. They don't even have to question whether they will use a tool that day. The habit is automatic. Why would they even consider not gaining knowledge or motivation that day? That would be like not eating or not breathing.

USING TOOLS SHOULD BECOME
A NATURAL HABIT

Many of the best leaders didn't start out automatically using tools. But they soon learned to. They listened to some of the tapes, read a book or two, and liked what they learned. Then, because they stayed with it, they began to notice something was happening inside of them.

They were changing. They were starting to think differently, react differently to problems, become more positive, and feel more self-confident and more willing to try some of the ideas they were hearing or reading about.

It's at that point that the serious distributor figures out a remarkable secret: that there's a direct relationship between *how much you use the tools*—and *how you think*, and *what action you take*. When you add *action* to *knowledge*, you get *success*.

If you've done this yourself, you know the next step is that you then make a *choice*—to make the tools an everyday *habit*. Congratulations! You've just opened the door that leads to your future.

TOOL RULE #3:
Tools aren't a negative *expense*; tools are a positive *investment*.

I've been studying people—especially the successful kind—for a long time. Yet it still amazes me that it's the people who are doing the *poorest* who complain the *most* about investing in themselves.

Instead of being proud about how much they're budgeting to set up their own future, they seem to be proud about how

little they're willing to spend on anything that would help! They value themselves so little that they refuse to spend the few dollars it would take to get the knowledge they need to improve.

THE WORST KIND OF POVERTY

This lack of self-worth is the worst kind of poverty; it wastes lives and ruins chances. It causes unknowing minds to *defend* their ignorance, instead of erasing it. It cripples enthusiasm and criticizes opportunity. It turns confidence to cowardice, and victory to defeat.

That's what low self-esteem does. And for the want of a few good *tools*, a family will falter—and a future will fail.

What a shame. That man, that woman, that family could have achieved so much. But the man, or the woman, who decided not to acquire the tools, said *it cost too much*. They and their families will go without the tools. In so doing, for the moment, they'll save a few dollars. And for the rest of their lives, they'll pay the price.

If you ever think twice about whether or not to invest in a tool, ask yourself this: "What am I worth?" If your answer is that you're worth a lot, then go ahead—acquire the tool and put it to use.

If, on the other hand, you ask yourself the question, "What am I worth?" and your answer is that you're *not* worth the investment, then *immediately* acquire the tool. You need it more than anyone.

WHAT DOES THE AVERAGE *"SUCCESS INVESTMENT"* TAKE THESE DAYS?

Don't let ignorant friends or a skeptical pocketbook kid you. If, as an example, you were to invest in a leading fast-food franchise today, the starting price would be $1,000,000 or so. Once you paid the money—or borrowed it and went to sleep every night hoping you could pay it back—you would then work harder than you have ever worked in your life.

You'd never see your kids, and when you did they'd be learning to flip hamburgers. You'd invest not only your up-front costs, but you'd eke out an existence year after year until your business started to pay you back.

You'd be physically or mentally on the job from somewhere around *3:30* in the *morning* until well after midnight. Seven days a week. 365 days a year. Every year.

Your accountant would tell you that if you kept up the pace, it might take seven years or more to even *begin* to get your investment back. But you put a lot into it, so you'd stay with it. You'd invest more of yourself than you ever thought possible.

And when you got there, you would have a nice tidy business. *Making hamburgers.* And still be working just as hard, with no end in sight.

Don't ever kid yourself about the tools or tell yourself you can do without them. You can't. Get them. Use them. They are the lowest priced investment you'll ever make, for some of the most valuable tools you'll ever posses.

Let me put it another way. The investments you make, for most of the tools you need, don't cost the price of a

hamburger *franchise*. They cost the price of a *hamburger*.

I've met a lot of people in your business who have a business today that is far bigger than any fast-food franchise. They weren't asked to buy a business or mortgage their family. But they did invest in every tool they could get their hands on.

They, too, worked hard. They took their business just as seriously as that other guy. They *used the tools*, invested their time, kept the dream, and refused to give up. And look what they have to show for it.

TOOL RULE #4:
The more you *use* the tools, the greater your chances for success.

Good tools give you good programs—positive program paths in the brain. But only if you use them. That's where you're particularly fortunate. You get the best tools that are available anywhere. And you get to use them over and over again.

You get to read the books, highlight the key points, re-read and reinforce. You get to watch the videos, see and hear clear, strong, visual and auditory messages, and then watch them again.

And then there are the cassettes.

There is no doubt that one of the principal reasons Amway has reached the size and scope it has—is because of the *audio cassette*.

Select any tool cassette at random and push "*play*," and see what you get! There is sheer brilliance in those tapes. Clear,

47

personal, edifying, intelligent direction. And vision. And motivation. And recognition. And belief. And experience. And support. And wisdom. And facts. And ideas. And questions.

And *answers*.

If you're not listening, you can't even begin to guess what you're missing.

CREATING A LIFETIME OF SUCCESS

You may not be aware that I chose, early on, to be a pioneer in the development of spoken-word, so-called "self-help" cassettes.

More than thirty years ago, I listened to the first self-improvement recordings I had ever heard. They weren't all that easy to use—at the time those messages were recorded on large, LP record albums.

But I liked what the messages said, and I had a young family with two small boys at the time, so I recorded the large, unwieldy, self-help records onto cassette tapes, so I could play the tapes when I was doing other things. In particular, I wanted to play the tapes while my sons and I were working on a project such as building model castles in the family room.

The far-reaching results of listening to those cassette "tools" was brought home to me again, not long ago.

My youngest son, Gregory, had graduated with a degree in Psychology from Arizona State University. He had then qualified for entrance into the Wharton Business School at Penn State, which by itself, is a tough job, and one that Greg was proud of.

We couldn't be together as much in person then, so we tried to make it up on the phone. One night, talking with Greg long distance, he said, "I want to tell you one of the reasons I've done so well in school."

I remember hoping he would say it was because I was the greatest dad in the world, and had taught him everything he needed to know. But what he said was, "Do you remember those tapes? You know, the ones you used to play at home while we were building model castles in the family room?" I told Greg I remembered, and then he continued.

"I don't know if I ever *tried* to think about them," he said, "but recently, since I've been in college, the things I heard on those tapes have kept coming back to me. Things about setting goals, and working at it, and living up to your best. I don't know why, but I remember them now, almost word for word."

And then he added, with a smile in his voice, "Of course, you made a difference too, Dad. But then, you listened to those same tapes."

The tapes my son was referring to that were helping him in college were the tapes he had heard playing in the background—*when he was five years old!*

A LESSON I NEVER FORGOT

When I went back to school myself, as an adult with a full-time career and a wife and two children, and working toward my goal of a degree in psychology, I was very busy. Because of my work at the time, I traveled a lot, and there were times I would fly home, drive from the airport to the small college I was attending, hand in my class assignments for the week, and fly out again that night or the next morning. (I had a very strong determination to reach my goal.)

But then I discovered a way to help me get through. Nearly overwhelmed with reading assignments and studying class notes, one day I took my cassette recorder to class with me. When the professor talked, instead of taking volumes of notes, I fed blank cassettes to the recorder. When I had a reading assignment—and it seemed like there were thousands of them—I read the material once, highlighted the key points, recorded those key points on a cassette tape, and went to bed.

ALL I DID WAS PUSH "PLAY"

Then, at night, instead of falling asleep sitting up, trying to read notes, or review the chapters again, I put the cassette in the player and pushed play.

I'll never forget the final exam I took in psychology that year. After the tests had been graded, the professor asked me to stay after class; he wanted to talk to me.

"I know you didn't cheat," he told me. "I know you're not that kind of guy. But what I want to know is, how did you remember the answers to the questions, *word for word*, in the same words I used during my lectures in class?"

50

I remember how I answered the professor. I held up one of my cassette tapes and said, "I have you here, on this tape." Then I lightly tapped the cassette on the side of my forehead, and said, "and now I have you *here*."

A SIMPLE SOLUTION THAT *WORKS*

Now, many years later, all students know about cassette learning. (Interestingly, many of them still don't take the time to use it.)

But teaching and training by way of audio cassettes, and then video, have been studied, endorsed, and utilized by every professional training organization that exists today.

So why is it that some students, and sometimes even people who really want to get ahead, will not take the time to listen to the knowledge that has been preserved for them—on cassettes and on videos?

I think I have an answer to this one. I believe the solution is too simple! The little audio tape is too practical, too inexpensive, and too *ordinary*. It's too easy to underestimate its value.

Perhaps if the simple audio cassette were priced the way the great Encyclopaedia Britannica is priced, we would respect it more. Perhaps if the simple cassette were heavier, made out of polished steel or burnished brass, we'd listen more carefully to the messages it held.

THE GREATEST CLASSROOM IN THE WORLD

Imagine that your bookshelf or study held the greatest personal development library in the world. Your own study, or your car, would then be the greatest classroom in the world. Of course, you don't really have to imagine that. If you're using the tools the way they *should* be used, that's exactly what you've got!

The books, the cassette tapes, the videos, and the other materials you have available to you right now *can change your entire life*. If you use them in the right way, they will also change the lives of the people around you—especially your family. That's not a simple hope or wish for you; it's a fact.

TOOL RULE #5:
Treat tools with the greatest respect. Tools give you knowledge. *Knowledge is your future*.

If you respect yourself, then you must certainly respect your own future. After all, your future is *you*, and who you *will* be, soon. The knowledge contained in those books and tapes and materials is knowledge that will become a part of you. Since the tools become a part of you, if you care about yourself, you'll care about the tools.

In this day and age, some families aren't taught much about respect and appreciation. But Amway families understand respect, both for each other, and for the people who add so immeasurably to our lives.

Real leaders work hard to give their gifts to you. Dedicated leaders work long beyond overtime to focus and present the knowledge that'll help you the most. If you sat at any of their tables, you would be inspired by their presence. If you could sit in their classroom, and be taught by them in person, you would be privileged.

I know that books and tapes, no matter how inspiring, often end up forgotten on shelves, gathering dust in the back of a closet, or in a box in the garage.

I would suggest another destination for tools of such importance as these.

Imagine that each cassette, each book, each video, each tool, is the *only one* on earth—and they are *yours* alone. No one else has them, and no one else can get them.

Stored within each of these tools, is the precise knowledge and guidance you need to move forward in the business.

If the tools you now possess were the only remaining copies, their value would suddenly become immeasurable. You would give them a place of prominence in your home. You would proudly show them to your friends, and carefully guard them from any harm.

After all, those tools hold the *knowledge*. They hold the *experience*. They hold the *answers*.

And now, in your hands, *those tools hold your future*.

TOOL RULE #6:
Tools are the keys that open the doors. *Make sure you use all the keys.*

Your sponsor can introduce you to the business. Your

upline will guide you every step of the way. Your mentor, if you've taken the time to find one, will help you make it.

But it will be the tools that take you there. It is the *tools* that day after day, night after night, open the door to your future. It is the tools that hold the door open.

That's because your sponsors, your upline, and your mentors and friends can care—and do everything they can when they're with you, or talking to you on the phone, or sending you an Amvox message. But when you're alone, and the door to the future starts to close, and *you're* all you've got, *you've still got the tools*.

It doesn't make any difference if you live in the middle of Virginia, or in the Iowa farmlands, or in California's Silicon Valley. When you're trying to build the business, and you start to feel alone, your population count doesn't always count—but your tools always do.

As your leaders so often tell you: Open one of the books and start to read, or pick up a cassette and push play.

Once again, *the door will open.*

HOW DO THE AMWAY TOOLS COMPARE TO THE TOOLS IN OTHER PROFESSIONS?

Professionals surround themselves with the equipment they need to be successful:

Successful astronauts have complicated control panels and the best equipment available. Successful chemists have the best-equipped laboratories money can buy. Successful marketers have endless focus groups and the best research consultants. Successful accountants use the best computer programs available. And successful Amway Distributors have the best, state-of-the-art, business development tools the industry has to offer.

You're just like the other professionals in the top fields. As an independent Amway Distributor, you're no different than they are.

The other professionals require—and take advantage of—the best tools of their trade—and so should you. They know they cannot survive or succeed without *their* tools.

As an Amway Distributor, you're a *professional*. *Your* tools are just as important to you as tools in *any other* profession. The only difference is, their tools usually cost a lot more. Their risk is a lot greater than yours. And your opportunities may reach a little farther than theirs.

USING THE TOOLS
CAN CHANGE YOUR LIFE

The tools you use in *any* business should require some investment on your part. It takes $10,000 to $20,000 annual tuition to attend many universities these days, and most professionals add thousands of dollars to their investment in ongoing training. Whatever your investment in your business tools is, consider yourself fortunate. By any comparison, you're coming out ahead. Anyone who doesn't recognize that you're getting a lot for putting in very little, has never had to pay for going through medical school.

No matter what you decide to do with the rest of your life, you ought to invest at least a year just using the Amway tools.

Why? Because the return on your small investment in using the tools could be beyond anything you could imagine. Just using the tools, say, for the next year or two, even if you weren't in the business, could change your life in some incredibly positive ways.

Now imagine what those same tools could do for you if you decide to take this business seriously.

WHAT TO DO:

1. Get out the tool list and take a new look. Check off every tool you'd like to have if someone *gave* it to you. Then divide the list into two categories: tools to get right now, and tools to get next. Then make a budget, get the ones you need now, and prepare for the ones you're going to get next.

2. Don't put it off. If you're not using all the tools you could be, no matter what excuses you make, you're really just avoiding success and wasting time. You're better than that.

3. If you have tools and you're not using them faithfully every day, set a goal to use the tools. Then use them.

4. Schedule the daily use of tools. If you are a married couple, work on this one together. If you're alone, and you're not reading and listening on a schedule, get out your planner and set a schedule. Use an ink pen, not a pencil.

Even if you're working hard and your schedule is tight,

don't let your schedule today sabotage your success for tomorrow.

Now that we've examined the course materials that Amway Distributor University provides for you, it's time to take a look at the other half of ADU: going to class.

*"You will never experience
a greater gathering of champions
than at an Amway function.*

*If you want to be successful,
you have to spend your time
with the people
who know how to succeed."*

Chapter Five

The Importance Of
Seminars And Functions

mway "functions" are so important that these seminars and large group meetings stand out as "super events" in the annual meeting schedule of every successful Amway Distributor.

When I studied your organization, on one hand I could see there was an exceptionally enthusiastic distributor attendance at all major Amway Distributor functions.

But at the same time, I recognized that some distributors weren't even attending these events. Or they were attending *some* of them, but not others.

These "other" distributors were missing everything the functions were providing—*they were staying home*—and I wanted to know why.

So I decided to carefully study the role of Amway "functions."

What I discovered about those who attended functions, and those who stayed home, led me to an important truth about your business, and more important to you, how you can be more successful in your business.

What I discovered about Amway functions was:

There are two kinds of Amway Distributors.

THERE ARE TWO KINDS OF DISTRIBUTORS: THOSE WHO *ATTEND FUNCTIONS—* AND THOSE WHO *DON'T*

I had been studying the attitudes and opportunities of Amway Distributors for some time before I decided to study the Amway *functions* themselves—and in particular, *who attended* those functions, and *who stayed home.*

I didn't make my observations by reading about your functions, or talking to attendees on the telephone. In the past three or four years I have personally attended, and spoken at, a great many of your functions.

During that time, I discovered some key differences between Distributors who attend functions regularly, and Distributors who don't. I've summarized the differences in two lists, as follows.

People who attend functions:

1. Are the most interested in getting ahead.

2. Are serious distributors.

3. Are couples who have figured out what it takes to get ahead.

4. Are having more fun.

5. Have learned what the functions are really all about.

6. Have planned and organized their time to attend.

7. Have budgeted and scheduled each function as an essential business engagement.

8. Plan to get a lot out of it—and probably will.

9. Take the opportunity to redefine their business activities and plans, and focus more strongly on their goals.

10. Will use the weekend event to learn more, redefine their goals, get motivated, associate with the best kind of people, learn to believe in themselves, take personal responsibility, and have an incredible, uplifting, and possibly even spiritually awakening time.

People who don't attend functions (regularly):

1. Don't really take the business seriously.

2. Let other things get in the way.

3. Think they can't afford to go.

4. Don't really understand what the functions are about, or what they really do.

5. Don't believe they can succeed in the business.

6. Are listening to someone else, someone *outside*, who tells them not to go.

7. Don't really believe in themselves.

8. Let trivial details or obstacles stand in the way.

9. Tell themselves they're just "too busy."

10. Don't really understand why they should go, or what the benefits are.

HOW DO YOU JUSTIFY SOMETHING YOU CAN'T *SEE*?

Some people have vision. They're blessed with being able to see beyond the limitations of the little things.

But most people haven't learned to have vision—to see beyond. So they only think most about what you *cannot* do, not what you *can*.

The average person continues to be average only because he lacks vision. He's incredibly limited in his thinking. And because he limits the way he thinks, he's one of the unfortunate people who can't see what he can't touch.

You can read the books, or watch the videos, or listen to the cassettes, over and over again.

You can *touch* the tools. But functions are different. You can't hold seminars and functions in your hands.

You can experience the function, for the most part, only while you're there. After that, you have to remember, and try to regain the enthusiasm and the spirit that you felt then, while you were there.

It's often easier to justify the investment in something you can hold onto.

Because seminars and functions are *experiences*, they could seem to be "here today and gone tomorrow," with no real value to you in the future.

DON'T LET SHORT-SIGHTED THINKING
LIMIT YOUR FUTURE

Books, tapes, videos, three-ring binders, business and educational materials—your family or your friends usually won't say too much about those.

But a three- or four-day *vacation*, "taking *time off* from work, traveling *how* far? to do *what?*" sometimes doesn't sit too well with the uninformed friends, relatives, and non-Amway "civilians" that surround you.

If you, or someone important to you in your life, thinks you would be better off not going to functions, it's a case of short-sighted thinking. It's time to refocus on the long-term benefits of attending.

63

Remember that just because you can't *see* or *touch* the value of going to every available function, that doesn't mean the value doesn't exist. It means you need to practice seeing the truth: that attending seminars and functions is one of the healthiest and most important things you can do for your future.

I've studied thousands of distributors at every level in your organization, and the facts are undeniable.

The people who succeed in this business attend the functions. The people who don't attend the functions don't learn from them, they don't grow, they don't get motivated, they don't reaffirm their goals, they don't stay in focus, they don't regain their perspective, they don't stay with it, and *they don't succeed* to the level they could.

WHAT TO DO:

1. Make the commitment. Start seeing seminars and functions as essential steps in your Amway business career.

2. Take every function or seminar seriously. They may be fun, but their lasting benefits are important and serious.

3. Never make excuses about why you can't attend. Spend the same amount of time working on your plan to get there.

4. Get out your planner and schedule every available event during the next twelve months. Then *go*.

64

If you have made the *commitment* to succeed in the Amway business, almost nothing will stop you from attending every meeting, seminar, and function that you can possibly attend.

Successful distributors attend every event they can. Instead of making excuses, they make it work.

The distributors who fail, fail to go to functions. The truth of attending your functions should be self-evident:

Those who make sure they attend every meeting and function they can, and take the business seriously, are the ones who get ahead.

Those who stay at home, stay where they are.

Part III
Getting Down To Business

"This is a very real business.
It's important.
It can help you succeed
beyond your greatest dreams.

If you take the business seriously,
it will change almost everything
you have ever imagined
about the rest of your life."

Chapter Six
Treating Your Business
Like A *Business*

Most Amway Distributors do a lot of things *right*. But in my research, I discovered there were a few simple—but important—things that some distributors were overlooking. And it's been affecting their businesses.

I also discovered that it's not just *new* distributors who make these mistakes—I've met people who have been in the business for ten years who are *still* making these same mistakes—and most of them don't know *why* their businesses aren't progressing.

**TREAT YOUR AMWAY BUSINESS LIKE A REAL
BUSINESS—IT *IS* A REAL BUSINESS**

I even found distributors who went only as far as having *business cards* printed—as though their name on a business card would prove they had *done* it—they could go to sleep at night saying, "I own a business."

What stops people from treating their Amway business with the same professional care they would give any *other* business they wanted to make successful?

My conclusion was that in other businesses outside of Amway, there is an *attitude* that's clearly a business attitude; there's a *place*—a physical space—to conduct business in, and there's a sense of having to take *responsibility* for your job or for the business you run.

In other businesses there's a routine structure to adhere to. The company you work for takes on the responsibility of creating the right environment. There's usually an office, or a workplace. In most businesses there are usually other people around—people who work in the same business.

And there are business plans, and meetings, and managers, and accountants, and planning and review sessions, and an organizational structure that is designed to make the business succeed.

MAKE SURE YOU'VE GOT THE RIGHT ENVIRONMENT TO SUCCEED

All of those create an "environment of influence." That's where your surroundings influence you and motivate you to think and act a certain way. In a business that's filled with the people and the sights and the sounds of a business, you feel like you're "in business," so you're naturally motivated to *do business*.

But that's seldom the case in a home. The *environment of influence* in a home has to do with family, eating, sleeping, relaxing, and so on, but it may not motivate you to do business. It wasn't designed to.

So you have to create the business environment yourself. That means that in order to manage a successful business from your home, you have to be *self*-motivated. Your businesslike *environment of influence* has to be one that *you* create *yourself*—starting with your own attitude, and then working its way into your physical environment as well.

SOME STEPS YOU CAN TAKE,
STARTING TODAY

To make sure you have the right "head space" for your business, there are some immediate steps you can take:

1. Always think of your business as a solid, long-term business.

2. In everything you think or say, always take your business seriously.

3. Make sure you associate with other people who will take your business just as seriously as you do.

4. Always think about and talk about your business as a full-time *profession*—not as a part-time hobby.

5. Always consider your business as being the most important career step in your life.

6. Visualize and discuss a clear mental picture of *you*, running the business and making it successful—and keep that picture in front of you.

None of the above steps will happen by accident. You have to take control of your own attitude about your business. You have to take it seriously.

YOU HAVE TO HAVE A *SPACE* FOR YOUR BUSINESS

No matter what your home, office, basement, spare bedroom, or garage space availability is, you *must* make a *physical space* for your business if you want it to prosper and grow.

This one is important because your *mental* space will always be affected by your *physical* space. Successful corporations know this; that's why you see so many gleaming chrome and steel and glass and granite buildings that are built for the sole purpose of giving people spaces to work in. The brain follows what the eye sees.

You could say, "Wait a minute. I'm in business for myself.

I'm independent. I don't need all that stuff."

But you do need a place—even in your home—that lets you know you're in business for real.

WHERE YOUR MIND GOES—YOUR BODY FOLLOWS

Remember, what you do most is determined by where your head is at most. So you need to surround your "business self" with the right environment of influence—the environment of actually being "in business."

Give yourself the space and the place to conduct your business as though you were getting ready to manage a million-dollar business. *You are.*

If you do this right, you'll be doing more than creating a physical space to work in. You'll be taking one of the most important steps you can take in learning *self-motivation.*

You will be creating a physical space and environment that motivates you to go to work, set goals, plan, take action, reach your goals, and ultimately, to succeed.

When you enter your "business" space, get ready to get motivated. When you enter that space, get ready to go to work. And always, when you enter that space, *get ready to succeed.*

CREATE THE RIGHT BUSINESS ENVIRONMENT

Make the space. Find the corner or the room, designate that space as your business space, and dedicate that space to treating your business like a business.

Make sure your business office includes all the items you need to run a *real* business: a desk, filing cabinet, telephone, in-basket, out-basket, stapler, note pads—even a computer and printer.

If you're just getting started and you can't afford to buy all those things at once, work at it gradually, but finish your space as soon as you can. The important thing to remember is to *create the physical environment* that will help you take your business seriously.

Literally *surround* yourself with your business. Don't just tack up a few dream-builder ideas you've cut out of magazine ads, and let it go at that. That's not a business.

Start by putting your next six-month business activity schedule on the wall. Next to it, put up your function calendar for the next twelve months, and write in your commitment to attend every available Amway function.

Next to that, put up your one-year, two-year, three-year, five-year, and ten-year goal plans.

And after you've had a serious meeting with your spouse and your family about it, post the exact date you'll go Diamond, and make sure you can't miss seeing it every time you enter your business space.

ALL IT REALLY TAKES
IS GETTING DOWN TO BUSINESS

73

If your old mental programs try to convince you to put it off, or tell you you're too busy right now, *write yourself a check.* Make it out for any amount you want—a quarter of a million dollars, a half a million dollars, or even a million dollars.

Or if your self-belief isn't up to it, go easy on yourself. Don't give yourself too much. How much can you handle—fifty thousand? Seventy-five thousand? (Personally, I would recommend you go for the million.)

But you decide. Then *write the check.* Write it out to you, fill in the amount, and sign it. And then fill in the date you commit to making that check good.

Put that check on the wall of your environment of influence—your business office.

Every time you look at that check, remind yourself that in order to one day cash the check, you have to take *personal responsibility* for your business. When you see the check, don't just glance past it. Stop for a moment. Look at it. Read the amount. Read the date. Then think about the action steps you can take right now, *today,* to build your business.

If you treat your business like a business, one day you can take that check to the bank.

"*Everyone you meet, find, or who comes into your life, could do even better by being in the business.*

Invite them in."

Chapter Seven

Overcoming The Four Fears Of Prospecting

O f all the areas of this business I have studied, no subject has created more questions, more concern—and more *opportunity*, than the subject of *prospecting*.

What is it that makes prospecting so intimidating for so many? Why is prospecting so easy to put off? Why would some people rather do *anything* than prospect?

As a distributor, you're taught all the *techniques* of prospecting, the specific steps to take, how to identify the prospect, what approaches to use, and you may even be taught word-for-word what to say.

But what we're going to discuss here is the *personal* side—the *psychological* side—of prospecting.

It's clear to me that you have good techniques and good professional steps to follow in the prospecting process. If you practice the techniques you're taught, you'll acquire the skills you need to prospect easily and naturally. It takes practice,

1. The Fear of Rejection.

Some fears are inborn, and others are programmed into us through experience—usually in our childhood. Inborn fears are designed to *protect* us or *help* us in some way. Programmed fears, that we weren't born with, aren't designed to help us, and they usually hold us back.

The fear of rejection is an inborn fear that's designed to help us. Here's a simplified picture of how it works.

To begin with, as part of this God-given miracle called the human brain, our brains come with a set of pre-programmed instructions. One of these instructions is that we're designed to naturally seek warmth, affection, and love. That insures us that we'll seek emotional environments that are safe and secure.

That same set of instructions has an opposite side; we're also designed to unconsciously avoid anything we believe will hurt us. Because of this deep, psychological protection mechanism, we're designed to *avoid* the enemy.

So we're designed to naturally seek those who will help us, and flee from those who would harm us. The fear of rejection is really the fear of something we imagine could harm us.

Medical researchers have learned that this natural, inborn capacity of the brain was designed to *help* us and *protect* us—that's part of the miracle of the brain.

WHAT ROAD SIGN ARE YOU FOLLOWING?

Imagine you're driving down a highway. Suddenly you come to a fork in the road, so you stop, uncertain about which way to go. Beside the road there are two signs, one pointing to the left fork, and one pointing to the right. The left fork sign says, *"Enemy."* The right fork sign says, *"Friend."* Which road would you take?

When you prospect, you face the possibility of rejection. That old fear center in the brain says, *"Enemy alert. Do not proceed."* Your own self-protect system is trying to protect you from an enemy that is, in this circumstance, *entirely imaginary*.

So what do you do? You take only the road that you know is safe, or you *stop* the car! You quit prospecting! And what stopped you from succeeding in the business was a very natural fear that protected you from an enemy *that didn't even exist*.

YOUR OWN *EMOTIONS* GIVE YOU THE *STRONGEST* DIRECTIONS

Getting stopped by imaginary fears happens when your *logic* is overpowered by your unconscious emotions—such as the fear of rejection. We all know there's no real harm, no personal danger, in being told "No."

"After all," our logical mind reassures us, "it's just a person saying no. It doesn't hurt me."

But our *emotions* tell us a different story: *"I can't take this rejection, it hurts me, and I don't like it when someone tells me no!"*

Your emotions are often stronger than logic, because

emotions create more *chemical activity* in your brain than logical thought does. When you put more chemicals into motion, you turn on more electrical circuits in your brain, so you make that message *stronger*—and the *strongest* message always wins out.

The fear of ridicule, or being made fun of, or laughed at, or being questioned, are all forms of the fear of rejection.

Whatever form this fear takes, the fear controls you if you don't control it. That can be hard to do if you don't even know what's happening—it's an *unconscious* fear in the first place. But once you know it's there, and what it really is, you can defeat it.

HOW TO TURN IT AROUND

The next time you have an opportunity to prospect, and you feel yourself holding back, think about it. Ask yourself the question, "*What am I afraid of?* Is it fear of rejection?"

If it feels like it might be, immediately give yourself some Self-Talk that turns the *prospect* into a *friend*.

If your brain is designed to avoid the enemy—or what it *imagines* to be the *enemy*—it will do everything it can to *avoid* it. The healthy way to counteract the fear is to immediately turn the prospect into the potential friend that he actually is.

When you think the word "prospect," what does your mind automatically tell you? Is your first thought immediately *positive* and enthusiastic, or is your first thought one of *uncertainty* or dread?

To defeat the fear of rejection, always practice seeing your prospects as the team who will build your future.

DEALING WITH THE *OTHER* FEAR
OF REJECTION—
THE FEAR OF THE WORD *"NO"*

As you might guess, the key to getting rid of the fear of the word "No" is up to your attitude. The stronger your self-esteem, the more self-confidence you create, the less any outside negative will bother you. The surest way to build your attitude—especially just before and just after you prospect, is to use Self-Talk, listen to high-energy tool tapes, and reread your goal plan.

Doing that helps you focus on what's really important. The "No's" you receive will come and go, but your business will live on long after them. If you're absolutely determined to make your business work, then nothing is going to stop you—least of all, hearing a "No."

TURNING "NO" INTO "YES"

The advice most people give you when it bothers you to be told "No," is to look at each "No" as one more step toward a *"Yes."*

While I agree with that advice most of the time, I also believe there's something you should do if you're being told "No" a lot. You should find out exactly *why* you're hearing too many "No's" in the first place.

It's normal to be turned down sometimes—at least until you've really mastered prospecting and showing the plan. But even until then, too many "No's" usually mean you're doing something wrong.

If that's the case, the solution is going to come from doing two things:

a. Learn from the best teachers you can get.
b. Practice.

If nothing's working, but you're still trying, you're probably practicing doing it *wrong*. Go back to square one.

Get advice from the distributors who have mastered prospecting. Listen to what they say, whether it hurts to hear it or not.

In summary, if your fear of rejection is stopping you from making the contacts and showing the plan, turn your prospects into your friends—before you even get to know them.

And if your fear of rejection is really the fear of being told "No" again and again, improve your skill and get better at turning those "No's" into new distributors.

2. The Fear of the Unknown.

Like the fear of rejection, the fear of the unknown is built into us at birth. It, too, is designed to protect us. It's the same built-in self-protect program that makes a toddler reach for its mommy when a stranger tries to pick it up, makes us nervous when we go on a job interview, or keeps us from walking into a dark alley, unprotected.

The fear of the unknown is an important protection system that many times in our lives has kept us safe, and probably more than once, has saved our lives.

But sometimes this self-protect program tries to protect us *too* much; it's supposed to remind us to be careful, but instead it stops us completely.

It's not supposed to do that to us, but sometimes our own self-protection programs don't know the difference between something that's safe—and something that's not.

PUTTING ONE FOOT IN FRONT OF THE OTHER

Fortunately, you can get past this one. You already have, millions of times. There was, sometime in the past, a first time for everything you do now.

Remember your first day at school? The first bus or airplane trip you ever took on your own? Have you ever moved to a new city, or started a new job? I know people who are nervous before they go to a party, simply because there will be people there they've never met.

But once you do it, and you're safe, your brain begins to form a new picture about that situation, or that person, or that job, or that prospect. The unknown becomes the known, and your brain tells you it's safe, you can relax now, it's okay to move forward.

THIS IS THE PERFECT TIME TO GET HELP
FROM SOMEONE *ELSE*

This is one of the unconscious fears that gives way to the moral support of someone else.

Having a spouse or a partner tell you it's okay is often all it takes to get you to square your shoulders, put your chin up, and step forward—pretty much like you might have done on your first day of school.

If your mom was there, she probably did her best to convince you that everything was going to be okay. She was doing something you still need today; she was *motivating* you. That means she was putting you into motion. And by just putting one small foot in front of the other one, you made it to the door of the school, into your classroom, and through the first day.

Your foot is bigger today than it was then, but the same principle applies. Use Self-Talk for your own self-motivation, and encourage your partner to give you *extra* motivation to *proceed*.

And then, put one of your feet in front of the other one. One step at a time, walk over to the telephone. Next, reach out your hand and pick up the receiver. Then, one number at a time, dial the number. After a few rings, the prospect will probably answer the phone. If he does, he will usually say "Hello." You can take it from there.

SEPARATE THE *JOB* FROM THE *FEAR*

85

If you don't know what to say next, then the problem is not an unconscious *fear*. If you don't know exactly what to say next, then your problem is *technique*.

Prospecting is a *skill*. Nothing else. If you want to do it well, you have to study the techniques, practice them, set a goal to build your skill, follow the plan, and get good at it.

Always separate the prospecting technique itself from the *fear* of doing it. Work on the prospecting steps by practicing them over and over. Work on the fear by recognizing it, overriding it, and moving past it.

3. *The Fear of Failure.*

This is a fear that's based entirely on believing we have to measure up to someone *else's* opinion of us. It's more than a fear of failing—it's a fear that tells us that we're not good enough, that we're inadequate, or that we don't measure up.

Nobody likes to feel like they're not as good as someone else. We don't like to think of ourselves as incapable, and we especially don't want other people to think we're inferior.

But the real problem is created by how we typically handle this fear. If we think we *can't* do something, our most natural response is *to not do it*. We would rather be questioned for putting it off, than to be proved inferior by trying and failing.

WHAT IF YOU'VE BEEN FOLLOWING A *FALSE* PICTURE OF WHO *YOU* ARE— AND WHAT *YOU CAN DO*?

86

The fear of inadequacy tells us we don't have the right stuff, that we weren't gifted with the intelligence or the right personality, or the right character. This fear lives at the core of who we think we are as individuals, and how we measure up. This is the fear that comes from having to face a truth about ourselves that we don't want to see.

So, of course, what's the *easiest* way around it? Some people give up, or they don't try in the first place.

Unlike the fear of *rejection* and the fear of the *unknown*, the fear of *failure* does not come with us at birth. We *learn* it. It is programmed into us by others, and then we, in turn, repeat those same false programs of inadequacy to ourselves throughout our lives.

So this fear is not one your brain needs in order to protect you or help you. In fact, there is nothing positive or helpful about this fear at all.

Of course, we all need to recognize what qualities we have that need improving, but no one is helped by looking in the mirror and thinking he's inferior.

Yet people often let this fear stop them because they don't understand it. They think they're not measuring up, when in fact they're measuring up just fine—*they're just using the wrong yardstick!* They're trying to live their lives based on the opinions of others. And that never works.

IMAGINE *NOT* BUILDING YOUR BUSINESS BECAUSE OF SOMETHING YOU *FEARED!*

I know distributors who stopped building their business

87

because they feared they would never become Diamonds. So, because they feared not making it to the top, they went *nowhere!* That's not a now-and-then problem. That's possibly the biggest problem you and your own downline will ever face in the business—letting your self-doubts and your unconscious fear of inadequacy stop you from building your business, and theirs.

The solution to this unnecessary fear is not in trying to tell yourself you're adequate—it is in letting yourself know that other people's opinions about you don't *count*.

Then move forward. Keep your eye on the goal, work the plan, and stay with it. You're smart, you're competent, and you have everything it takes to succeed. You're better than adequate, you're a *champion*. And don't ever forget it.

4. The Fear of Work.

Before you think this fourth fear of prospecting sounds odd, or simply something a parent might say, let's look at what the fear of work really means. It may be the most important fear of all to overcome.

When you fail to do something you think you ought to do, it's almost never because doing it is too hard. "Work" doesn't have to mean something is difficult, or drudgery, or even physically tiring.

As an example, if you play tennis, you probably put out more physical effort in a game of tennis than you do in a whole day of work. Or if you take your family camping—the kind of camping where you find and cut the firewood for yourself—you'll expend a lot of energy, but it really won't be work. Or if you exercise, work out, or ride a bicycle, you'll burn more calories in the gym or out riding than you will in the office.

WHAT IS YOUR FIRST THOUGHT—WHEN YOU THINK OF *"WORKING"* FOR A LIVING?

Unfortunately, we've come to view anything connected with "working" for a living, as *difficult, tedious*, or *tiring*. Exercising, or playing, on the other hand, is called "exhilarating," or "invigorating." It's a thrill to feel so tired!

That would suggest that the only difference between "work" which means going to a job, and "effort" which could mean having fun on a weekend, is all up to your *attitude*—how you *think* about, and what you *feel* about, the activity you're "working" at.

The best way to define what is "not fun" work, and what is "fun" work, is this: One of them you *have* to do, and one of them you *don't*.

And yet, *not fun* work is work you usually get paid to do, while *fun* work is usually something *you* pay to do. (For most people, it costs money to have fun.)

What all this means is that the fear of work stops many people from *working* their Amway business, and *succeeding*, because they mentally put building their Amway business in the *not fun* work category, instead of into the *fun* work category.

THERE IS A GOOD REASON WE DON'T LIKE THE WORD "*WORK*"

Our first impression of what it means to "work" is based on the feelings we have about our *jobs*.

Even people who like their work would usually love to do better, if given the opportunity to do so. In fact, most people, if given a check for, say, $1,000,000 on Monday morning would probably think about quitting their jobs on Tuesday—or *Monday afternoon*, if they were sure the check would clear.

Most of us, in the quiet, honest parts of our mind, would rather be doing better than we are now. It's not that we don't want to work. It's that few jobs will ever give us the life and the freedom that we have the potential to live out. In fact, most jobs fall short of helping us excel at all.

WHAT DO MOST JOBS REALLY DO FOR YOU?

Most jobs don't *enrich* your spirit; they *deplete* it.

Most jobs don't add *excitement* to your life; they fill your life with *tedium* and *boredom*.

Most jobs don't *motivate* you; they demand instead that you stay in line, and do exactly what someone *else* expects you to do.

Most jobs don't help you *grow* daily, day after day; they define you instead as some number or classification—and expect *you* to fit *their* mold.

Most jobs don't give you *an unlimited future*; they give you a *ceiling* which is little above *average*, and hope you'll be happy with the plaque or the watch when you retire—*if* you last that long with that company.

Most jobs don't give you *independence*; they *restrict you* to someone *else's* time line on what you should be doing with your life.

Most jobs don't give you true *security*; they pay you—for now—and promise you a future that lasts only until the paycheck and the promises are no longer any good.

Most jobs don't give you real *hope*—they only get you to hope that you'll get your next paycheck, or that you'll get a raise, or get to keep your job.

Most jobs don't give you *control over your own future*; they give you nothing more than the opportunity to serve someone else—someone *else* who is in control of *your* life.

STARTING TODAY, GIVE A NEW MEANING TO THE WORD "*WORK*"

It's no wonder we don't like the word "*work!*" It doesn't

sound fun or fulfilling. In fact, to most people, the word "*work*" sounds like the opposite of the word "*freedom.*"

Most work *is* drudgery, and takes us *nowhere*. But from here on out, when it comes to building your Amway business, if you change the meaning of the word *work*—to the word *freedom*—you may never fear this word again.

If you have ever hesitated to prospect, take heart. This is one challenge you can conquer. Always remember: The *techniques*, you can *learn*. The *fears*, you can *defeat*.

It's only when you're not aware of the problem, or what's causing it, or what to do about it, that this problem can stop you. But once you know what the problem is, what caused it, and what to do about it, you can get past it.

WHAT TO DO:

1. Defeat the *fear of rejection* by constantly letting yourself know that the *prospect* is your *friend*.

2. Defeat the *fear of the unknown* by putting one foot in front of the other, and *always* taking the next step.

3. Defeat the *fear of failure* by never again basing your belief in yourself on the limited beliefs of others.

4. Defeat the *fear of work* by always remembering that when you are building your Amway business, *work* really means *freedom*.

If there's a single step you can take now, to make prospecting a natural, comfortable, easy part of building your business, it'll be for you to see your fears for what they really are.

They are nothing more than your own imagination believing in old doubts, and trying to stop you from reaching your dreams.

Your fears are nothing more than shadows in the night. They never really hurt you.

And they go away when you turn the light on.

*"Choose to succeed, believe that
you can, have the faith
to see it through,
and always make it your goal
to share that success
with everyone you meet.*

*If you want to do something
important with your life—*

Show the plan!"

Chapter Eight
Showing The Plan

Once you've overcome your fears of prospecting, and you've extended the invitation, and your prospect has accepted, something *else* happens: now you have to *show the plan*.

For many distributors, those three words are among the most terrifying in the language.

The problem often masquerades as a fear of public speaking—but that's almost never the real issue. The truth is that when it comes to *showing the plan*, most distributors are not absolutely certain that they'll "do it right," or that they're "good at it."

How about *you*?

How good are you at showing the plan? Would you classify yourself as "*Expert,*" "*Average,*" or "*Beginner*?"

Whichever category you fall into, your determination to become an *expert* at showing the plan could have an important effect on your future.

To help you judge your skill level, answer the questions in

the following short quiz. If you're working with someone, you may even want to discuss your answers with your partner.

RATING YOUR SKILL AT SHOWING THE PLAN

1. **When showing the plan, what do you do *best*?**

    a. _____

    b. _____

    c. _____

2. **When showing the plan, what do you do *least* well?**

    a. _____

    b. _____

    c. _____

3. **How would you rate *how well you know the information* you're presenting?**

    ☐ Extremely well
    ☐ Generally well
    ☐ Just "okay"
    ☐ Not too well
    ☐ Not well at all

4. When you're showing the plan, are you:

☐ Nervous
☐ Relaxed
☐ Calm
☐ Excited

5. When you're showing the plan, how would you rate your *attitude*?

☐ Always warm
☐ Sometimes warm
☐ Always cool
☐ Sometimes cool
☐ Friendly

6. When you're showing the plan, how would you rate your *confidence*?

☐ Highly confident
☐ Hopeful
☐ Uncertain
☐ Discouraged

7. When you set an appointment to show the plan, how would you rate your *punctuality*?

☐ Always on time
☐ Early
☐ Occasionally late
☐ Always late

8. **When you show the plan, how would you rate your** *appearance*?

   ☐ Very sharp and professional
   ☐ Casual
   ☐ Could be neater
   ☐ Sloppy

9. **When you show the plan,** *how closely do you follow the exact wording* **of the presentation?**

   ☐ Word-for-word
   ☐ Sort of
   ☐ Not very closely

10. *How often do you ask your upline or your mentor for help* **on improving your presentation?**

    ☐ Frequently
    ☐ Almost never
    ☐ Never

11. *How often do you practice* **improving your presentation skills?**

    ☐ Frequently
    ☐ Only when presenting
    ☐ Never

12. **How do you think your *prospect* would rate *you* at the end of your presentation?**

   A. Professionalism:

   ☐ Very professional
   ☐ Could be sharper
   ☐ Not very professional

   B. Knowledge:

   ☐ Very knowledgeable
   ☐ Unsure of some of the facts
   ☐ Not very well-informed

   C. Sincerity:

   ☐ Very sincere
   ☐ Somewhat believable
   ☐ Not very sincere

   D. Effectiveness:

   ☐ Very convincing
   ☐ Somewhat effective
   ☐ Not very convincing

   E. Confidence:

   ☐ Extremely confident
   ☐ Average
   ☐ Nervous and uncomfortable

Now that you have a general idea of how well you do when you show the plan, let's take a look at how you can learn to do it better.

In the next chapter, we're going to cover three specific steps you can take to improve your presentation. Regardless of how well you did, or didn't do, on the "Showing the Plan" quiz, these three important steps can help.

"When you show the plan,
always imagine
you're talking to someone
who is going to go Diamond.

You never know
when that will be true."

Chapter Nine
Three Important Steps To Improving Your Presentation

T here are many people who prospect well, and show the plan often, but they sponsor little. When I heard about those people, I began to wonder how someone could show the plan several times a week for several weeks in a row, and still not sponsor people into the business.

It's difficult for me to imagine anyone being shown the plan, without wanting to become a distributor.

Yet, on one hand, there are some distributors who show the plan many times before they sponsor a new distributor, while on the other hand, there are distributors who sponsor almost every prospect they show the plan to. And both of them are presenting the same plan.

IF IT ISN'T THE PLAN, IT COULD BE YOU

It's clear that something is wrong with the presentation that some distributors are making. If someone *else* is showing the same plan *you* are, and they're sponsoring more than you are, then you could be doing something wrong.

And that's good news, because it means if you fix the problem, and do it right, then you'll soon be sponsoring just as many people as the other guy.

I wanted to know what it was that some of the distributors were doing wrong, and what it was that the other distributors were doing right. Here's what I found.

In each case, the distributors who were the most successful in showing the plan, were taking three "extra" steps that were missing with the *un*successful distributors.

These key steps had little to do with the technical side of the plan, or the business side of the plan. The steps they took had to do with *themselves*, their own *attitudes*, their own *motivation*, and their intense *desire* to succeed.

I also found that although these steps were essential to success, none of the steps was difficult—anyone who wanted to follow the steps could do so.

If something has been missing from your presentation, even though you've been using all the right words, you'll probably find that following these same steps will fix the problem.

STEP #1:
PUT YOUR BELIEF IN GEAR

The best presentation always begins with your *belief.*

To even *think* about showing the plan, you have to begin by shifting into high belief.

With this plan, you *can* believe. All the facts are on your side: The Amway plan is logical. It makes sense. It is sequential—that is, every point you make always leads to the next logical point. The math works. The story of Amway and its success is a fact. The potential is there, waiting for the right distributor to take advantage of it. And above all, *the business works.*

But your belief has to be stronger than just trusting the facts. There's more to this business than the numbers and the dollars and cents.

YOU'RE GIVING YOUR PROSPECTS AN INCREDIBLE GIFT

To show you what you're really offering to your prospects, let's say you went to Philadelphia and visited Independence Hall. Imagine the curator ushering you in. Once you're inside, imagine him carefully picking up a beautiful old parchment from its glass case and handing it to you. Imagine holding in your hands the most important document in America's history, and perhaps the most important formula ever written for the freedom of man. Imagine holding the *Declaration of Independence* in your hands.

You would hold it gently, not wanting to harm it in any way. That single document, and the words that were so carefully penned on the paper, offered a new life, and a new freedom for all.

THE LIFE AND THE FREEDOM
YOU OFFER NOW

What if, in the spirit of that great Declaration of Independence, *you* could hand someone *else* that same kind of message? What if you could place in someone else's hands, the formula for freedom?

You would hold it carefully, present it with respect, and treat it with the knowledge that the words you shared were changing the world.

That's exactly what you're doing when you present the Amway plan.

Your Amway business is what the original Declaration of Independence was all about. If you haven't read it recently, you should. It offered "life, liberty, and the pursuit of happiness" to the brave new world. When you show the Amway plan, you're not presenting some marketing idea; you're presenting good people *the chance to declare their independence.*

With Amway, the spirit of free enterprise is alive and well. It offers independence, freedom, and a chance to build that brave new world.

Two centuries ago, the world changed because of a plan. Today, more than two hundred years later, the world is changing again. Back then it was just called America. It had borders.

Today it is called Amway. And this time it has no borders. This time the message is being heard around the world.

That is the kind of gift you're giving to your prospect each time you show the plan. *Believe* in what you're giving them, and your skill will begin to improve.

YOUR MOST IMPORTANT ASSET IS YOUR PERSONAL *BELIEF*

It isn't how perfect your speaking skills are that counts the most. It's how much your prospect can see you believe in the business. Your absolute, unstoppable *conviction* in what you're saying is the first step in making a successful presentation.

Let me give you another example. Let's say you had received an inheritance of some worth. Among the papers you inherited, you found what appeared to be a map to a fabulous treasure.

To be certain that the map was genuine, you take it to an expert in maps and treasures, and to your surprise, you discover that you indeed own a map to one of the world's great treasures.

You've studied everything the map told you, and you couldn't help but notice that the treasure map was very clear in its instructions: in order to find the treasure, you must take someone with you.

So the scene is set. The treasure you've been hoping for is waiting for you. All you have to do now is share the secret with someone else—and together, you'll find the treasure, and the unlimited future that treasure offers.

THE AMWAY PLAN IS A MAP TO YOUR FUTURE—AND TO THEIRS

Imagine holding that marvelous map to your future in your hands. Imagine the incredible possibility of sharing that opportunity with the person who will help you find the treasure and make the dream come true!

It really *isn't* a story that's too good to be true.

When you were given the Amway plan, you *were* handed a clearly-drawn map that would take you to the greatest treasure you can imagine. But to own the treasure, you have to trust someone else, someone who will help you find the treasure.

If the map you held were an ancient treasure map, you would *immediately* begin to think of the prospective individuals you might choose to help you find the treasure.

The name we often give to the "prospective" individuals who will help you own the treasure, is a name that fits. They are called "prospects."

With the Amway map, the more prospects you have, the more fortune you will find. The more people you show the map to—*the more prospects you show the plan*—the faster your business will grow, and the sooner all of you will reach the treasure.

YOU'RE NOT *SELLING* —YOU'RE GIVING THEM THE CHANCE OF A LIFETIME

Some people, new to the business, still think that when they're presenting the Amway plan, they're *selling* something.

Let's get this one straight. So that you never again have the false notion that you're "selling" anything by showing the

107

plan, I'd like to make this point so clear you'll never forget it.

When you're showing the plan, you're doing something entirely different from selling.

I've identified a substantial list of contributions you're offering to your prospect's future when you're showing the plan. What follows are just a few of them:

1. When you show the plan you are: Giving your prospect a chance to succeed in life.

2. When you show the plan you are: Offering the opportunity of the attainment of true financial freedom.

3. When you show the plan you are: Offering your prospect a plan of achievement that has been tested, practiced, and proved for more than *thirty years*, and over *three generations*.

4. When you show the plan you are: Sharing an opportunity that may be the most positive, worthwhile *"chance at life"* your prospect has ever known.

5. When you show the plan you are: Offering a potential *future*, and a potential *fortune* to someone who, otherwise, would have had neither.

6. When you show the plan you are: Giving *life* to people who thought they could go nowhere.

7. When you show the plan you are: Giving people a chance to succeed—when otherwise, they wouldn't have known they could do it for themselves.

8. When you show the plan you are: Helping every prospect rise above the average, make something of his or her life, and giving each of them a way to make it work.

9. When you show the plan you are: Helping people build self-confidence and self-belief. For some of them, you'll be giving them a gift that, without you and the plan, they would never have found.

10. When you show the plan you are: Above all else, giving people the gift of *freedom*. What you add to their lives will never be measured. The freedom you offer them has more value than a treasure chest of silver and gold.

Your most successful upline distributors have shared the treasure map. They've found the treasure for themselves, because they've been willing to share the opportunity with others.

So they take that all-important extra step. They make the decision to *believe*. They share that belief with everyone they meet.

And when they show the plan, *they put their belief in gear*. That's why they're successful.

STEP #2:
MAKE YOUR AMWAY BUSINESS YOUR **MOST IMPORTANT** *BUSINESS.*

You'll never make a first-place business with a second-rate attempt.

If you want your Amway business to be big, then you have to put it in first place; not *after* it makes it, but *now*, so that it *will* make it.

Some distributors think they'll devote their full attention to their business *after* it's successful. I know it doesn't make any sense to think like that, but people do it all the time.

WHAT DO YOU WANT TO END UP WITH?

If you want your Amway business to be the kind of business that's bigger than any other job you could ever have, then you have to make building your Amway business *more important than your job.*

If you do, you'll end up with an *incredible business.* If you don't, you'll end up with your *job.*

All successful distributors practice this second vital step in building their business. And it's one of the most important steps you can take in making presentations that work. Why? Because your prospect can spot your commitment the moment you walk in the door.

If you haven't made your Amway business your #1 career, how can you possibly expect your prospect to take you or your business seriously? *Why should he*? You're not even taking the business seriously *yourself.*

And that's the single most important downfall of failed presentations:

110

You're telling someone else it works, when your own track record tells him it doesn't. It isn't true, of course; the business works great, but *he* doesn't know that. All he has to go on is the impression he has of *you*.

So your prospect gets a completely false picture of the potential of the business, because anyone can see that you aren't committed *yourself*.

Unless, of course, you *are*. If you *are* committed, if Amway *is* more important than your job, more important than any other career, your prospect will know it. He'll see it in your eyes. He'll sense it in your poise. He'll feel it in your energy. He'll hear it in your voice. When you meet someone who is 100% committed to this business—*you know it!*

MAKE YOUR AMWAY BUSINESS
MORE IMPORTANT THAN YOUR JOB—
AND WATCH WHAT HAPPENS
TO EVERY PRESENTATION YOU MAKE

When you sit down with your wife or husband, have a serious Amway business meeting, and say to each other, "*This is it*. As of this moment, our Amway business is more important than our jobs," your presentations will reflect that commitment.

And with your stronger commitment, you'll immediately begin to find more value in the time you spend building your skills. You're no longer investing in a part-time also-ran; you're now investing in the most important business and career path of your life.

111

Suddenly, your investment becomes worth it. So you spend more time learning the business, more time getting help and advice, more time practicing, and more time learning how to be more and more successful.

Now, showing the plan even feels different to you. It should. When you show the plan, you know you're building your future, and it shows.

Learn the steps, study the distributors who do it right, and follow the plan. That will open the door to the opportunity.

But beginning now, make your Amway business more important than your job. Nothing lights the fire like *commitment.*

STEP #3:
ALWAYS, ALWAYS, ALWAYS BE A PROFESSIONAL.

There is simply no replacement for a professional manner. Your bearing, your appearance, your choice of words— everything about you communicates a message.

If the message your style communicates is that you are a person of *quality, manners, integrity, responsibility,* and *knowledge,* then you'll communicate that you're a professional. But if you're sending *different* messages than those, your level of professionalism—or *lack* of it—will affect every presentation you make.

Learn to be a professional in every way, and watch what happens to the success rate of your presentations.

No one wants to join a business run by people who aren't professional.

How would you feel if your doctor acted unprofessionally?

112

What if he was shoddy, untidy, used bad language, or never had on a clean shirt? I'd go to a different doctor. Or what if your accountant acted like he never made it through math? Or the captain of the airplane you're about to board looks like he partied all night?

None of us wants to do business with someone who doesn't look and act like he knows what he's doing. He has to look the part. And the sharper he looks and acts, the better the chance we'll want to do business with him.

WHAT KIND OF IMPRESSION DO *YOU* MAKE?

How is your appearance? *Neat, sharp, professional?*

What kind of language do you use? *Proper, respectful, educated?*

How do you talk? *Intelligently, clearly, thoughtfully?*

How do you stand or sit? *Poised, confident, self-assured?*

What is the look in your eyes? *Interested, alive, aware?*

How are your manners? *Considerate, proper, always appropriate?*

How organized and in control are you? *Organized, on top of things, in control?*

How is your presentation? *Sincere, direct, clear, experienced?*

Wouldn't you like to be in a business team with someone who looked neat, sharp, and professional . . . who used language that was always proper, respectful, and sounded educated . . . who spoke intelligently, clearly, and thoughtfully . . . who was poised, confident, and self-assured . . . who

113

always looked interested, alive, and aware . . . who was always considerate, proper, and appropriate . . . who was organized, on top of things, and in control, and who presented his or her ideas in a sincere, direct, clear, and experienced way?

I know I would. And so would your prospect.

Why? Because we have more *trust* in someone who has his act together than someone who doesn't. And if you're going to commit your future and your career to something, the last thing you want to do is to do business with someone who doesn't have his act together.

The people you invite to join you in your business want to deal with a professional. They want to *trust*. If they don't trust, they'll go somewhere else. Or they'll say no. Or they'll tell you they're going to "think about it."

EVERY SKILL OF "PROFESSIONAL STYLE" CAN BE *LEARNED*

The skills that go into the makeup of professional style are some of the most basic social skills of all—and some of the easiest to learn.

But some people just weren't told those skills might be necessary, or important, so they didn't spend much time practicing them. Most people have one or two of these basic skills that could use a little work. But no matter how many of them you have that might need some work, don't be discouraged for a moment.

Just start practicing them. Start by playacting them, even if you've never practiced them before. Most of us know at least some of the basics. And anyone can learn them and get good at them.

Don't rely on old advice that might have told you you don't have to act like a professional to succeed in this business. Look around you. The top distributors in the business have all learned to be professionals, and they're among the finest business professionals you'll meet.

Many of them will tell you they weren't that way when they started in the business; they *learned* the skills. And so can you.

A CHECKLIST OF
YOUR PROFESSIONAL STYLE

You probably have many or most of these simple skills and habits mastered already. But just in case you'd like to brush up on your professional style skills, here's the basic list:

□ *Your General Appearance*
When you're working your business, prospecting, or showing the plan, what is your overall appearance? The important question is, do you always look professional?

□ *Your Grooming*
This one may be obvious to you, but some people don't recognize the importance of a clean-cut professional look. It can make an amazing difference in how your prospect

perceives you, and how he perceives the business.

☐ *How You Dress*

Your clothes don't have to be the most expensive, but they should reflect a professional look. That doesn't mean you have to buy a whole new wardrobe you may not be able to afford at the moment. But always make sure your apparel is neat, clean, and appropriate to the occasion.

If you're going to talk to people about being successful, you should dress the part.

☐ *Your Alertness*

Some people miss this one entirely. When you're doing business, others unconsciously watch for signals that will tell them how sharp you are.

Keep your eyes alert, show you're interested in everything that's going on, let them know you're alive, aware, intelligent, and professional. The more you practice being alert, the more intelligent people will think you are.

☐ *Your Posture*

People tend to sit like they think, and think like they sit. The same is true of the way we stand and the way we move. People who are slouching or too casual give off signals of being careless or casual in their thinking and in their business.

When you're in a business situation—especially when you're showing the plan—always be aware of your own *physical* attitude. It will tell your prospect what your *mental* attitude really is.

☐ *The Words You Use, and the Way You Speak*

116

Your words, your use of language, your vocabulary, and your style of speech will tell your prospect a great deal about you. The problem isn't that people don't know how to present themselves more professionally when they talk—it's simply that they don't polish their speech habits as carefully as they polish their shoes.

All speech is a matter of *habit*. We all have some *good* speech habits and some *bad* speech habits. If you want to be successful, learn to practice and use only the *good* ones.

☐ *Your Manners*

If ever there was a reason to mind your manners, it's when you're building your Amway business. Nothing takes the place of courtesy, deference, and respect, when you're establishing a business relationship. It's up to you to *always* use the best of your grooming—and there's *never* a moment when it's okay to forget your manners.

Quality manners are a sign of a quality person. And they are *always* a part of being a professional.

☐ *Your Work Habits*

Your upline has no doubt counseled you on your work habits. Good work habits help you build a business; poor work habits stop you from reaching the goal. But just as important, when you practice good work habits, it *shows*.

Your prospect can see it from the moment you walk into the room. If you're totally on top of your business, he's going to know it, and your presentation will be more effective.

Creating good work habits isn't something you should do now and then. Creating good work habits is a lifelong activity of anyone who wants to succeed in the business.

117

☐ *How Organized You Are*

Your Amway upline is great at teaching you the value of personal organization. If you're not in control of yourself, you'll never be in control of your business. Real professionals learn to get organized. And how organized you are will never be more obvious than when you're showing the plan.

☐ *Your Focus*

This means how well you pay attention and how well you stay on track. When you're showing the plan, if you cover your discomfort by wandering off, ad-libbing, or getting distracted, you'll take your prospect, and the plan, right off track.

A professional sticks to the subject at hand, keeps his focus, and puts all of his energy into his presentation.

☐ *Your Punctuality*

This is one of the prime skills a true professional perfects. It probably shouldn't have to be mentioned; everyone knows it's bad business to be late—but some people do it several times a week.

Some distributors lose their prospect before they have even begun—simply because they weren't courteous enough—and *professional* enough—to be on time.

This skill has an unbreakable rule: *Never, ever, be late.* If you have an appointment to show the plan, and you're a professional, you'll be on time.

☐ *Your Honesty and Integrity*

Your character is defined by the integrity you practice.

How direct you are, how honest, how sincere, how trustworthy, and how professional, will always be the result of how much integrity you build within yourself.

It's integrity that lets you look at yourself in the mirror, and see someone you respect. It's your integrity that lets your prospect look you in the eye, and see someone he can trust.

□ *Your Presentation Style*

You weren't born with a presentation style. Whatever style you have now, you learned. Whatever style you'd *like* to have, you can *also* learn.

You probably know at least one distributor (if not several) who is so practiced, his style so professional, he makes showing the plan seem like the easiest, most natural thing you could do. It can be the same way for you, if you work at it.

Watch carefully how the successful distributors show the plan. Study the styles that are the most professional. *Learn* the style just like *they* did. Your own personality will still come through, of course. It will still be *your* presentation. But it will be *professional*.

□ *Your Attitude*

Your professional demeanor begins with your *attitude*. If your attitude is always professional, your actions, your appearance, your habits, and your style, will follow.

To have a professional attitude, you have to practice thinking like a professional. To do that, spend time with professionals, read what is written by professionals, listen to the tool tapes—and *study* them as you listen.

Don't let your thinking settle back into *average*. Keep pushing your own attitude upwards. Talk to yourself. Discuss your professional attitude with your mate. Surround

119

yourself with a professional environment of thoughts and actions.

Where your mind goes, the rest of you will follow.

YOU'LL IMPROVE MORE THAN JUST SHOWING THE PLAN

There's a real value to you in practicing these basic skills. The first is that getting better at them will help your business. And they'll help you in more ways than one.

Your presentations will go better, and you'll bring more distributors into the business. You'll radiate more confidence and begin to build more trust. You'll attract top quality people to your team—like attracts like—and your business will grow.

But above and beyond that, when you practice these skills, they start to become automatic. And then that wonderful thing happens. One day you look in the mirror, and you smile back at yourself. You did it! You got better! And nothing takes the place of the kind of self-esteem you have given to yourself.

It's a great gift—from you to you. And it's a gift that will stay with you for the rest of your life.

WHAT TO DO:

Step #1: Put your belief in gear.

120

Step #2: Make your Amway business your most important business.

Step #3: Always, always, always, be a *professional*.

If you spend time reviewing and working on what we've discussed in this chapter alone, you'll gain new insight into showing the plan—and I predict more success for you.

Focus on these three "extra" steps that the successful distributors have mastered. These three steps alone have made the difference in many of the most successful businesses; they could mean the turning point for your business as well.

What encourages me most about these three extra steps is that they're not complicated. In fact, they're quite simple, and virtually anyone can follow them.

I hope you do what the successful distributors have learned to do. Practice the steps. Go Diamond.

*"Choose to believe
in the good things in life.*

*Build your business
and make your life work.*

*You only have time
for the positive."*

Chapter Ten
What To Do About Negative People

Several years ago I began writing a series of stories on self-esteem for children. The stories are about Shadrack The Self-Talk Bear. Shadrack came to Earth from the planet Excellence to teach self-esteem to little Earth kids.

In those stories I introduced the terrible "Negatroids." Negatroids are shadowy, almost invisible, ghost-like creatures who whisper negative things into the ears of little children, and try to make them bad.

In the stories, the terrible Negatroids can also disguise themselves to look like *friends*, and *parents*, and *teachers*, and other *adults*, and even news reporters on television.

Unfortunately, I'm afraid there are an awful lot of Negatroids around these days. Only they're not just whispering bad stuff into little kids' ears—they're trying to get *us* to believe them too.

So it's no wonder that one of the questions I'm asked most often is what to do about people who are negative.

What *can* you do about the Negatroids?

THE PROBLEM WITH NEGATIVE PEOPLE

I can only imagine the number of people who have failed in their Amway business because they let someone who was negative get to them.

People who are negative can be the end of any good thing. Their own fear, low self-esteem, and self-doubt create failure in life—for themselves and for the people around them.

What to you is a *dream*, to them is a scheme. What to you is a *chance*, they think is a dance. What to you are great *tools*, they think are for fools. What you work to *achieve*, they cannot believe.

And to that description, you can add: *And when the treasure is found, they'll be nowhere around.*

LEARN TO IDENTIFY THE TWO KINDS OF NEGATIVE PEOPLE

In building the business, there are two kinds of negative people you can run into. The first kind are those people who are *un*informed or *mis*informed—they don't know anything about the business, or they don't know the facts—so they put it down because they don't know any better.

We meet people like that every day. They don't understand the business, so they make fun of what you do, or they try to make you look bad for doing something good.

The second kind of negative people you run into are those who are negative as a way of life—and they're negative about just about everything.

What these people have in common is that they both form a picture about the business that's *inaccurate*. One because he doesn't know the truth, and the other because he has limited thinking—he disapproves of *anything* that's upbeat and positive.

Part of the secret to your success is in identifying *which* kind of negative person you're talking to. They might look alike and sound alike—they may even say the exact same things to you. But their *reason* for questioning the business or saying negative things is completely different. You can help yourself by knowing which is which.

A. People who are negative because they're *un*informed or *mis*informed.

These people you can help—if you're skilled enough to get them to listen. These are the people who may have a good attitude about a lot of things. But they have to be shown.

These people may sound negative, but they're really just communicating the fact that they don't know enough about the business to make a truly intelligent decision. Some of these people think they know it all already. Some of them have been told things that aren't true. Some don't know anything about the business, and they admit it. But all of them should stay on the list of good prospects.

125

These are people that are worth working with. Keep talking. Keep communicating. Keep informing. If they're at all open-minded, and if you're practiced and sincere in your presentations and when you talk to them, they'll get the facts—and see the opportunity.

B. People who are negative as a way of life.

These people are a different story.

Even if you try, you can't, by yourself, change people who are negative as a way of life. You can encourage them, and you can try to help them build their self-esteem by the way you treat them. But when it comes to being negative or not, people have to make the change for themselves.

This kind of negative person may also often be misinformed about the business, so he might look like that's his only problem—when in fact his bigger problem is that he's generally negative about everything.

A TRULY NEGATIVE PERSON SEES ALMOST EVERYTHING IN THE SAME NEGATIVE WAY

This kind of negative person sees things very differently from the way other people see things.

Because he's a pessimist, he misses the point. He doesn't see life as being full of wonderful possibilities; he sees life as full of nothing but problems. He thinks the world is out to get

126

him, take advantage of him, and take what little he has away from him.

People who are always negative aren't trying to single you and your business out for something to be negative about. They're negative about *everything!* With these people, their negativity has become a habit.

PEOPLE WHO ARE TRULY NEGATIVE ARE AFRAID TO TRUST THEMSELVES— OR ANYONE ELSE

To them, *anything* that looks good is viewed with suspicion. You'll often see the same kinds of negative attitudes in their marriage and their relationships, in their job, in their attitudes about their future, with their associates, and even with their children.

To the truly negative person, nothing looks safe. He doesn't trust himself; he's unsure about his own success, so how can he be sure about anything?

The result is that he's suspicious, and critical, and unsure of almost everyone. He's convinced that every good idea is a trap of some kind, and he's afraid he'll get caught in it.

He doesn't realize that it's precisely *because* he's negative that nothing works for him. He doesn't realize he's doing it himself!

The truly negative person doesn't accept that *he's* the one who's responsible—so instead of taking responsibility for his own failings, he blames everybody else. Underneath it all he is angry, fearful, mistrusting, and convinced that something will always go wrong. And, of course, for him, it usually does.

So what does he do? He takes it out on everything around him—and, not surprisingly, he doesn't believe in your business, and he probably thinks you're crazy.

Why doesn't he believe you when you present him with the truth about Amway?

He can't. He's too busy defending the small patch of ground he calls his life, so limited by his own fear and low self-esteem that he can't believe in anything that could change his life for the better.

What does he do instead of seeing the dream, getting on board, working hard, and making his life work? Look at these symptoms of a negative person who is approached about becoming a distributor—or who may even *be* a distributor who's still negative:

He complains about the cost of getting in.

He complains about the time it takes.

He complains about attending functions.

He complains about the cost of tools.

He complains about how much work it takes.

And, of course, right from the start, he's convinced that the business can't work.

Instead of finding the good, and creating some *success* in his life, he complains about *everything*, and forces himself to fail. He looks for the bad, convinces himself he's right, and then tries to prove it to the world.

WHAT TO DO WHEN NEGATIVITY IS
A WAY OF LIFE

There *is* something you can do.

You can learn how to deal with negative people so they don't pull *you* down *with* them. When you're building your Amway business, that's important. People who are negative as a way of life don't have vision. Because they're limited by their own attitude, they can't see the dream—so they try to bring *you* down to *their* level.

When you meet someone who is negative about most things, you can be sure he'll be just as negative about what you have to offer. Go past him. Don't let him pull you down.

He's wrong, and he doesn't know it, but trying to convince him isn't going to change his mind about the business. Remember, he has trouble believing—*really* believing—in *anything* positive.

Your enthusiasm and your belief in the business just makes him more convinced that it couldn't possibly work—at *least* not for *him*.

DON'T TRY TO BE A THERAPIST

Could this Mr. Negative be turned around? Possibly. If he took the time to get rid of the old mental programs he's got that tell him life doesn't work. But that's not your job. And if he doesn't want to change, he probably won't, no matter how much someone else tries to help him.

You're not a therapist; you're a professional business person building your Amway business. There are plenty of other people who'd like to make something of themselves. Don't spend your time trying to save those who refuse to hear—spend your time building your business instead.

DON'T LET *THEIR* NEGATIVITY
SPREAD TO *YOU*

The most important thing you can do when you run into someone who is truly negative is to protect your own attitude from theirs.

Negativity rubs off. People with a bad attitude can inflict it on others, just by being around them. But, if you're going to succeed in this business, you can't just ignore everyone who might turn out to be negative—you at least have to give people the opportunity to be positive.

If someone looks a little negative at first, it could be a "Negatroid," or it could be someone who just needs more information.

Here are the rules I recommend following when you're dealing with negative people:

●   **Always start by giving everyone the benefit of the doubt.** Good people care about others. Part of caring about others is expecting the best from them. Start by giving people the chance to prove they're positive and have a healthy mental attitude.

●   **Look for the telltale signs that will tell you whether the person is *only occasionally negative*, and possibly uninformed or misinformed, or *negative as a way of life*.**

130

Do they smile frequently, or do they frown? Do they listen openly, or shake their head or look skeptical most of the time you're talking? Does their general manner make you feel good about them, or do you feel edgy and defensive when you're around them?

We've all seen the signs, but if you *practice* being aware of what they *mean*, you'll be able to handle the situation better.

● **Stick to the facts.** Don't get led into a disagreement or having to defend yourself. Let the facts of the business speak for themselves. And other than your own great attitude, keep your emotions out of it.

● **Make sure your own attitude stays "up."** This doesn't mean you should show false enthusiasm. People can see it—and *negative* people can spot it a mile away.

● **Always remain confident.** Remember, you know you're right, regardless of what someone else says. You have the facts; they don't.

● **Don't try to convert people who are negative as a way of life.** If you discover the person you're talking to is really Mr. Negative, don't try to give him a brain transplant by convincing him you're right. He's been negative for years. He's not going to get over it by listening to your presentation.

● **Don't invest in failure.** If people are truly negative, won't believe in facts, and choose to be pessimistic, that's their option. Once you've determined that's their pattern, don't invest any more time trying to persuade them to change.

131

● **Always give yourself strong, positive Self-Talk before and after spending time with a negative person.** Arm yourself with good Self-Talk: *"I no longer live my life based on the negative opinions of others. I choose to keep my attitude up. I feel great, and I'm creating success in my life!"*

● **Reread your goals.** If you've been in an especially negative situation, read your goal sheet out loud, more than once if you have to. Nothing will keep you on track better than a confident attitude and a strong renewal of your determination to reach your goals.

● **Never, at any time, let someone else's attitude get you down.** You have to be strong on this. Talk to yourself. Keep your own attitude up, smile (use a mirror if you have to), and don't let anything cause you to lose a minute of this precious life you've been given.

Practice using those rules every time you talk to someone who might be negative. Above all, remember you've got a job to do, and it's up to you to keep your spirits up and your head held high. After all, there are a lot of people counting on you. Most of them are future distributors you haven't even met—yet!

WHAT CAN YOU DO WHEN THE NEGATIVE PERSON IS SOMEONE CLOSE TO HOME?

132

Sometimes the problem lives closer to home. I know it can be especially difficult when someone close to you is negative. It could be your wife, or husband, or even your parents or someone else in your family.

Almost all negative personalities come from getting negative programs when we were growing up. Whatever messages got typed into our "mental computer" most often, are the programs that create our attitudes today.

So if someone got a lot of negative programs as a child or even as a young adult, that person probably still carries those mental programs today. Unfortunately, our thoughts, actions, and attitude always reflect the strongest programming we got.

Those programs determine our self-esteem, what we believe about almost everything, and in particular, how successful we think we can be.

It's no surprise, then, that people who got too many negative programs along the way, wind up becoming negative themselves.

You can't change the programs of every negative person you meet, but there *are* some things you can do to deal with the negative person at home.

HELP THEM BUILD THEIR SELF-ESTEEM
IN EVERY WAY YOU CAN

The key to helping them is to help them build their self-esteem back up where it ought to be. It isn't that they're not quality people with as many talents and capabilities as anyone else; it's just that they can't *see* themselves that way.

133

They'd like to, but their own vision is dimmed by old programs that tell them they're not as good as someone else, or life is unfair to them, or they're just not born to be special, or things don't work out right for them the way they do for someone else.

They don't see themselves as excelling throughout their lives. They simply don't have the picture of themselves being exceptional, or successful. And when they *do* see a picture of success, they aren't in it.

SOMETHING YOU CAN DO EVERY DAY

If someone you care about is negative, you can be sure that person has self-esteem that's been injured somehow. It has to be built up. You can help by always showing them good pictures of themselves, and always encouraging them.

That can be something as simple as the little things you say to that person each day. Instead of fighting the problem and telling them what's *wrong*, even a simple, but vital, change to telling them what they're doing *right* can make a difference.

If you use Self-Talk, especially if you listen to Self-Talk cassettes, play those tapes quietly in the background where the other person can hear them. Don't tell them they ought to listen, and don't make an issue out of it. The tapes will do what they're designed to do, on their own: they'll give the listener a whole new set of positive programs to put into practice.

Let that person know you believe in him. Tell him so,

every day. Say the words, *"I believe in you"*—and mean it.

Start telling the person, *"You're special,"* or *"You really did that well,"* or *"You're incredible!"* any time at all, and do it often, without waiting for a special reason.

For people who aren't used to it, that might sound odd at first, but keep doing it anyway. We all need to hear things like that. Negative people need it especially.

DON'T EXPECT OVERNIGHT RESULTS

People spend years getting negative programs, so don't expect them to change overnight. It won't take as long to build them back up as it did to tear them down, but it can take months, or sometimes longer. The secret is in staying with it long enough for the new programs to take effect.

Keep in mind that success builds success. Each time they do something that makes them feel good about themselves, give them a reward—a few words, a note, a gift, a smile, a nod of respect and approval—to let them know they just created a minor success.

The more little successes they have, the better they'll feel—and the more they'll be willing to try it again. In time, with enough little victories in building their self-esteem, the process starts to happen almost automatically. Eventually, the old negative thought patterns—the old programs—begin to be replaced by the new programs.

Helping someone in that way, of course, takes love, and a lot of caring, and a certain amount of patience. But if that person is worth it to you, then so is the effort it takes.

And when he, or she, looks at you, and smiles one of those wonderful "I did it!" kinds of smiles, and you see that self-esteem shine through, no one will even have to thank you for what you did. That smile will be thank-you enough.

WHAT IF THE NEGATIVE PERSON IS *YOU*?

If you notice that you yourself feel negative or unhappy a lot of the time, then it's time to do something about it.

I want to encourage you in this. Over the years I've known many people who started out negative, but ended up positive, healthy, and happy. In other words, they *did* it!

What they did for themselves was exactly what they would have done for anyone else who was negative. Instead of helping the *other* person build his self-esteem, they had to work on their *own*. The steps are exactly the same. But this time you're talking to you.

Negativity robs you of your birthright, your right to live and achieve, and your right to succeed as a human being. Negativity diminishes your spirit, dampens your enthusiasm, and darkens your day. It destroys your vision and defeats your dreams.

And all for nothing.

Of any human emotion, none is more destructive and has less worth than negativity. It has no value in a mind that strives to be healthy, and no place in a life that wants to succeed.

I find negativity so much the opposite of what is good and

136

healthy that to every degree possible, I refuse to let negativity into my life or into my home, even for a moment.

WHEN IT COMES TO *YOUR* ATTITUDE— *YOU HAVE A CHOICE!*

It comes down to a choice. You can choose to see the world full of light, and hope, and opportunity, and good—or you can choose to see the opposite. Whichever you choose, there are two truths you should always be aware of:

The first truth is that *the one, enduring ingredient that insures success more than any other, is optimism.* Optimism is the belief that you *can*.

The second truth is that *belief is a choice.*

If you'd like to get rid of any negative attitudes within you, your first step is to believe that you can.

If keeping a healthy, positive attitude about the life you have in front of you is a choice, then building that attitude is ultimately up to you. This is one thing *you* can definitely do something about.

DON'T EVER LET A NEGATIVE ATTITUDE STOP *YOU*

You're too important to let negative thinking—*yours* or anyone *else's*—stop you. You've got too much to do, and too much to live for.

I've met the distributors, the families, the children, whose lives have been changed in countless positive ways by this business. I've seen what it can do.

If someone like you hadn't refused to give up, those people wouldn't be in the business today—and their lives wouldn't be enriched in so many ways.

There's a whole world out there waiting for you. Where *you're* headed, you don't have time for imaginary fears and worn-out excuses. Where *you're* going, things are changing fast, and you're an important part of what's happening.

THERE'S A LIGHT THAT'S SPREADING THROUGHOUT THE WORLD

Take a moment and look at the cover of this book. Notice the light that's rising over the Earth.

That majestic oncoming glow on the horizon is Amway, bringing the light of life, and hope, and a new future to people everywhere—people who, without Amway, may have had no real future at all.

You're doing that. *You're* changing lives. *You're* making a difference that counts. *You're* going to a future that's alive with opportunity, filled with optimism, and powered by results. *You're* going to a place called "*Success.*"

How many people with negative thoughts and negative minds can say the same for themselves? How many of *them* will stand tall, and be counted, and let their success be an

138

example for others to follow?

No . . . they'll just sit by the wayside, trying to find fault with others, because they've failed to find what's right in themselves.

Don't give their limited ideas and unfounded fears one more moment of your time. *It's time to put the fears and doubts aside.* It's time you got rid of them for good.

Where *you're* going, you're not going to need them.

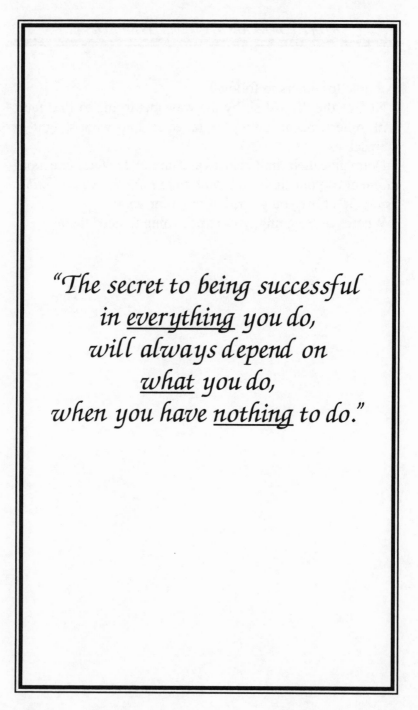

"The secret to being successful
in <u>everything</u> you do,
will always depend on
<u>what</u> you do,
when you have <u>nothing</u> to do."

Chapter Eleven
The Hidden Enemy That Can Sabotage Your Business

T here is something that is stopping us from achieving our goals—both personally, and as a nation. It is something that's destroying our kids—and it isn't just drugs, and it isn't a joke.

It's something that's robbing us of our time, stealing our strength, and undermining our ambition. It's something that is so ordinary, so "every day," that we hardly even think of the effect it has on our lives. It's something that influences our thinking, consumes hours of our thoughts, and programs our minds in a negative way.

THE PROBLEM THAT DESTROYS LIVES— AND COUNTLESS AMWAY BUSINESSES

This problem is not a questioning public, or negative family members, or even the fear of prospecting. This problem is far greater than any of those.

This problem lives in our homes, talks to our kids, steals our minds, pretends to relax us, programs our thinking, robs us of our self-esteem, and is the most dangerous addiction that we face today.

Perhaps by now you've recognized this enemy of personal growth and success. It's a word that's so well known to us that we consider it to be a part of our lives. It's so important to us that when it's questioned, we think the question is a *joke*. But this time it isn't a joke.

You have, right now, something in your home that is more threatening to you than anything the outside world could send to defeat you. It is not your friend. It is probably your greatest enemy.

Its name is *television*.

And it is trying to destroy *you*, your *family*, and your *business*.

TELEVISION, BY *ITSELF*, DESTROYS LIVES, PROGRAMS ATTITUDES, AND KILLS AMBITION

I hope you take every chapter in this book seriously. But I hope you take this chapter *especially* seriously.

The speakers at your functions who have said, "*Turn off the TV,*" as they delivered their messages to you, were saying something important.

But let me take it beyond that message. I'm going to tell

you more than just to turn off the TV—I'm going to tell you *why:*

INVITING A THIEF
OF THE MOST *DANGEROUS* KIND
INTO YOUR HOME

I grew up at the same time television came into our lives. I saw it grow from a curiosity to a lifestyle. One day only a few people had a television set in their living rooms—and suddenly, in just a few years, most homes had television sets in every room of the house.

I considered myself unlucky when my parents made the decision to not allow television in our home. I thought my father was being too strict, or uncaring. But one day, when we'd asked again why we couldn't have a television set when everyone else had one, my father gave me an answer I wouldn't forget.

"How would you feel," he asked, "if I invited a thief to come into our house and take away everything that makes us happy? Would you think I was a good father if I did that? That's what would happen if I brought a television set into our home. It would steal the most valuable things we own."

My father meant it. Television would have robbed my family of the most precious qualities we possessed. But he was true to his word, and my brothers and sisters and I grew up without once having a television set in our home.

We still ate meals together. We talked to each other in the evening. We did our homework, or played games together.

We read a lot. We were always reading something, or writing something or learning something, or doing something creative. But we never watched TV.

Meanwhile, in homes all around us, everyone was turning on the television more and more. I watched my friends and their families change their lives because of that box in the corner. They stopped eating meals together. They stopped talking to each other—you know, *real* conversation.

Most of their discussions were about who got to watch what. They stopped reading almost entirely. And even their schoolwork often lost out to the competition of the television set.

They thought we were odd, and they often made fun of us. But the thief had invaded their homes, and it would never leave again.

IT TURNED OUT, MY FATHER WAS RIGHT

I still, then, thought it was unfair, never getting to watch television like everyone else. But that was before I learned how the human brain works, and how it gets programmed, and how we live our lives based on the programs we get.

It would be much later that I would even begin to understand the full impact of what television "programming" was having in the lives of the people who were watching it.

Neuroscientists have learned that every single message you and I have ever received, is recorded, or "programmed," into actual physical pathways in the brain. Every message your brain has ever gotten, from birth on, is still there.

Everything you've ever heard is recorded in those pathways. Everything you've ever seen. Everything you've ever said. Everything you've ever done. Everything you've ever experienced. Everything you've thought.

It's all still there, *permanently recorded,* in millions of neural circuits—pathways—in your brain.

What makes this important is that the researchers also discovered that the programs you and I have right now that are the strongest, are the programs that literally determine *what we think* and *what we do,* every day.

WHAT KIND OF PROGRAMS
IS TELEVISION *REALLY* GIVING US?

Now think of those families all sitting down in front of their television sets, but imagine that every message their brains are receiving is being recorded in special pathways in their brain. And then, imagine that the brain is designed to *act* on the programs it has that are the strongest. *It is.*

Now consider that during the school years alone, the average child watches more than *18,000 killings* on television.

Imagine the families watching other families on TV that are not families at all, but broken homes.

Imagine the number of times a school kid witnesses the use of drugs on the television set, or watches criminals and crimes, or sees kids shout at their parents, or watches endless images of a whole society breaking down.

And then ask yourself, "Where are our kids getting their 'programs?' Where are you and I getting ours?"

Remember, the human brain is designed, neurologically, to operate like a very powerful computer. It always ends up playing back what you put into it.

So why are our families breaking down?

Why are we losing our values?

Why are drugs a problem in grade school?

Why are there so many teen pregnancies?

Why are gangs commonplace in every city in the country?

Why are more students failing or dropping out of school than ever before?

Why are parents unable to manage their kids?

Why have we lost sight of the bright, happy future we once thought was in store for us?

We are playing back the programs we got given to us—on that harmless screen over in the corner, with its little remote control, and its total control of our lives.

THE KIND OF ACTIVITY
THAT DESTROYS YOUR *BUSINESS*
AND YOUR *POTENTIAL*

Let's say that on some particular evening, instead of showing the plan or working on building your business, you plop down into your easy chair, reach for the remote control, and hit the "on" button. Two or three hours later the evening is over, and nothing happened.

146

Or did it?

Something very important happened. And it wasn't good.

In that two or three hours you *practiced* doing nothing, while at the same time, you literally programmed your brain with whatever you happened to have watched on TV—in itself, a frightening thought.

You didn't just break even. You programmed yourself to go backwards. You took no action on your business, when you could have taken action. You gave yourself several hours of programming that was at worst, negative and destructive, and at best, mindless.

But it didn't stop there.

You also lowered your self-esteem. (We think less of ourselves when we do not achieve or add value to our lives.) You also very likely made unconscious excuses. You set a questionable example for the other members of your family to follow. And you may well have just missed starting a new leg.

The plan you didn't show, was preempted by a television show you shouldn't even have watched!

WHAT ABOUT THE *GOOD* PROGRAMS ON TV?

When I suggest to people that watching TV is holding them back, those people almost always tell me that TV is actually okay, because there are *good* programs to watch, too.

The favorite examples of "safe" TV are usually PBS, A&E, The Discovery Channel, The Disney Channel, and The History Channel. I believe that makes *five* channels out of about *150* or so channels now available on cable.

But let's be realistic. Of the total number of hours your television set is turned on, what percentage of that time is actually devoted to the "good" programs? Half? A third? Less?

And if you're like most people, you turn the set on early for a program you want to watch, and *leave it on* long after the positive program has ended.

A few good programs do not justify the destruction of a nation. The opportunity to watch a program on archeology is not what is destroying America! It is the endless hours of mindless programming that infiltrates the days and weeks and lives of almost every American man, woman, and child from the time they get home from the hospital as an infant, to the day they die.

And with the opiate of television, they live that life without ever *once* living up to the incredible potential they could have achieved in area after area of their lives.

But, at about two days old, they come home from the hospital, ready to be programmed, and *there it is*. The television set. Oh, I forgot. There was a television in the hospital room. And it was turned on.

IMAGINE SPENDING THAT SAME EXACT TIME CREATING A *LIFE*

Just imagine what your life could be like if, instead of getting all of those thousands of hours of intense mental programming from watching TV, you would instead use that same time to give yourself an incredible mind, and build an incredible business.

Can you imagine what you would *know*, if you had spent the same time actually studying something valuable, instead of just sitting in front of the TV?

Can you imagine what gifts you would give to your family if you spent that same time doing something *worthwhile* with them?

Just imagine what kind of a home you might be living in today, if you had spent every hour you sat in front of the TV set during the past four or five years, showing the plan or building your business, instead.

ARE YOU RESTING, OR *RUSTING?*

"But," you could say, "I need that time to rest."

Are you really sure about that? Is it really the rest you need, or is it the escape? Or is it that you now believe you *need* the time in front of the television, because it's a habit you've come to accept?

What has happened is that television has seduced us into thinking we have it tough, and we're too fatigued, and we *need that TV*. It is an addiction as strong as any drug. And it is just as harmful. The truth is that the more we can be led to watch TV, the more time we'll spend watching the *commercials*, and that is, after all, what television is really about. Selling us something.

So they have to get you to watch it. And the best way to get

149

you to watch it isn't to give you stimulating programming—it is to condition you to believe that you work too hard, and you should rest; *you should watch a little TV.* And then a little more. And then a little more.

IF YOU WANT TO IMPROVE YOUR BUSINESS—AND YOUR *LIFE*, TURN OFF THE TV!

Convincing people to take control of their lives, and shut down the TV, is a difficult idea to sell. TV itself does a far better job of persuading you to watch than any of us who would persuade you to turn it off. But then, television is part of your life—it's there, and it lives with you every day of your life; we don't.

But I'll try to persuade you anyway. And here's why.

If I had to give you the one, final, and most important secret for making your business work, for keeping your kids away from drugs, for making your marriage the best there is, and for creating financial independence for the rest of your life, it would not be a secret just about the business. It would be a single idea that could, beginning today, begin to change your entire world for the better. It would be:

Turn the television set off.

In my professional work I study human programming. I know how the chemical and neurological processes work in the brain. People who study this field have learned that there is a *direct* link between the mental programs you receive, and what you do with your life.

I also know that when the television is on, *it* is in control of that incredible neurological programming process in the pathways of your brain. And I know that most of the programs you receive when you're watching TV, on any average night, are exactly the *opposite* of the mental messages you need to have in order to excel.

CAN YOU BREAK THE HOLD?

When we watch TV, we're literally *paying* others to program us—and usually with the worst. We're hiring someone to hold us back, and very possibly, messing up our kids for good.

Why do you suppose our kids, even little ones, are shooting each other in school? Why do you imagine teenagers can listen to rap, and then believe that it's good to hate cops? Why do you think the institution of marriage isn't even considered sacred by millions of young people and adults today?

It is because television has programmed our nation.

In fact, it worked so well that you might not even consider breaking its hold. You may come up with reasons that prove to you that television is really okay.

You may justify a need to keep your television attached to your life. You might even think that this "programming the brain" stuff is just talk, and nothing more.

You may believe that your kids are just fine; nothing to worry about there. And you may tell yourself that television is not really to blame for apathy, wasted time, the loss of our values, the breakdown of the family, the destruction of initiative, and the loss of our vision as a society.

If you do not choose to turn off the television, and break its hold, then you'll know that what I told you was true. You'll know just how strong television is. And if you don't turn it off, then television *wins*. And *you* lose.

WHAT IF YOU WERE GIVEN FOUR FREE MONTHS IN A YEAR?

I mentioned in a previous chapter that some people complain about not having enough time to build their business—it takes too much time away from TV.

Imagine what you could do if someone were able to suddenly give you *four extra months* in a year! Certainly you could use the time to build your business much faster, get caught up on things, get organized, plan more, and *still* have extra time left over.

Well, you *can* have four extra months in a year if you'd like to. All you have to do is take two hours that you would have spent watching television each day, and put that same time to practical use. Here's the math:

Multiply two hours a day, by 365 days in one year. That equals 730 hours. Now divide the 730 hours by the 40 hours of a typical work week. That equals just over 18 extra forty-hour weeks a year, or just over *four extra months*—free!

Some people watch three hours or more of television a day.

152

They would gain *six months* of their time back—an entire *half a year* of workdays they're now spending in front of a television set.

People who are in control of their lives don't spend what amounts to four, or five, or six months parked in neutral and going nowhere. Only most people don't notice it because they just do it a few hours at a time, day after day. That's how people *fail*, just a little each day—day after day.

You deserve better than that. And so does your business.

YOUR BUSINESS DESERVES THE BEST CHANCE YOU CAN GIVE IT!

Because your Amway business is so important, it deserves every chance you can give it. Even if you weren't in the business, I would suggest that you shut down the TV, but if you *are* in the business, you're going to see an even greater change in your life when you pull the plug.

It'll be like breathing a whole new breath of life into your business. You'll feel less tired, you'll accomplish more, your self-esteem will climb, and because you're putting more of your time in the right place, your business will grow.

The law of cause and effect works both ways. If you fill your time and your mind with the wrong ideas and the wrong actions, you'll follow the wrong road. Your own future will be impaired because of it.

But if you fill your time and your mind with positive activity—showing the plan, and building the dream, your future will show it.

153

So change the cause. Shut down the television. *Show the plan instead.* And enjoy the effect.

Long after the kids have stopped complaining how dumb it is to turn off the TV, and long after you've gotten over the withdrawal symptoms yourself, the real results will begin to come in.

After all, you'll have your home back. You may have your family back. And most certainly, you'll have a big part of your *life* back.

YOU CAN DO IT. YOU CAN *WIN!*

The fact of the matter is, it's difficult to stop watching TV only if you're not committed to improving your life. If you want to have the benefits of not watching television, you have to be committed.

It will take some explaining, some educating, some goal-setting, some dream-building, a clear plan, some real rewards, and some determination.

But in the end, if you make the commitment, and stick to your guns, you will win. And when you do, your family will know it, your life will show it, and your business will grow.

Part IV
Building Your Belief

"*Every day*
you have another chance
to build your future.

How many dreams
will you dream today?

And what will you do
to make them come true?"

Chapter Twelve
The Positive Power Of Dreambuilding

T he skill called dreambuilding is one of the most important reasons why Amway is successful. What dreambuilding *appears* to be, at first glance, is the practice of making a wish-list of sorts, finding things you might like to own that only wealthy people get to have, and then imagining owning them yourself. But *real* dreambuilding is a lot more than that.

The basic idea is to focus on specific goals, visualize them, see yourself working hard to get them, and one day—owning them yourself.

I like that idea.

But if you'd really like to dreambuild—that is, if you really want to build the dreams, and make them come true, there are some things you can do that will help.

DREAMBUILDING IS A *SKILL*

The first thing to learn about dreambuilding is that you have to learn how to do it. It doesn't come naturally. We don't just wake up one morning and say, exuberantly, *"I want a castle, I want to tour all of Europe, I want a personal weight trainer, I want a Rolex watch for every day of the week, I want to quit my job and never work again!!! . . ."*

We don't even automatically demand time for ourselves, or set goals to go back to school, or believe that we can ever have the time to raise our kids, one-on-one.

For many people, living those dreams doesn't just *happen*—and few of us even expect those kinds of things in our lives.

Unless we learn how to build dreams.

And set goals.

And take action.

And see the dreams come true.

AMWAY SHOWS YOU HOW
TO BUILD DREAMS

All of that starts with something that is one of the greatest gifts the Amway business will ever give you. It will show you how to build dreams.

That doesn't mean foolish dreams or impossible goals or impractical plans. It means dreambuilding. Putting a picture of your own future in your mind, letting you see yourself achieving that goal, and then equipping you with the tools you need to make that dream come true.

If I were given the task of helping someone's life today, along with the skills of self-reliance, taking personal responsibility, setting goals, the willingness to work, and the willingness to have faith, I would teach that person the skill of building dreams. Why?

Dreambuilding is an incredible, practical tool.

Dreambuilding is something you can learn to do.

Dreambuilding is something that has rules, or guidelines that anyone can follow.

Dreambuilding is something anyone, with practice, can get good at.

Dreambuilding is something you can practice.

Dreambuilding is something you can perfect.

In short, Dreambuilding is a skill.

GET GOOD AT THE SKILL OF DREAMBUILDING
AND YOU'LL GET BETTER
AT BUILDING YOUR BUSINESS

The problem is that most Distributors I've met believe that dreambuilding is an "experience," a "visualization process," "something you do at functions," or something you do "now and then."

But real dreambuilding is bigger than that. More important than that.

Dreambuilding is an everyday way to realign your thinking from the *old* way—to the *new* way.

Not just in the car you drive, the watch you wear, the clothes you can afford, or the square footage of the house you live in.

The visualization of success is more than pictures in your mind of things you want to own. Success, in every way, is a picture of you, and your life, that you *choose* to create—every moment of every day.

Yes, the drive in the new Cadillac helps. Yes, imagining yourself owning the beautiful home, is important. Yes, seeing you and your spouse spending some of the most incredible days of your life in the Caribbean or on Peter Island, is a good picture for you to build.

But remember, too, that dreambuilding is also knowing you choose to live without ever having to worry about paying the bills. Dreambuilding is being able to go to a movie on Tuesday, at two in the afternoon. Dreambuilding is not working for someone else—ever again.

Dreambuilding is seeing yourself living a life of quality and substance—choosing where you live, choosing what you do, and choosing *your* future for yourself.

DREAMBUILDING ISN'T "WISHFUL THINKING"; IT IS SEEING COMPLETED PLANS IN ADVANCE

There is not a single, truly "great" individual you can point to who did not dream—plan, visualize, etc.—his or her dream in advance. It wasn't wishful thinking; it was *planning*—with an advance *picture* of the completed project.

Long before I held a completed copy of this book (the book you're now reading) in my hands, I held what *looked* like a completed book. It was empty. For many weeks, months before this book was finished, I was able to hold a special "far in advance" copy. I could look at the cover and see the picture of the sun rising, cresting over the Earth, like a new morning for all mankind.

During that time, the cover showed me the victory of Amway, spreading over the Earth, like the dawn of a bright new sun, shining brilliantly over an incredible world, bringing light out of darkness.

That is a metaphor, a mental picture, but it was exactly what I wanted the book itself to do. I wanted every current Amway Distributor, every leader, and every *prospective* distributor to see Amway in the "light" of this new dawning.

Before I had written the first word of this book, I had sketched that cover.

Long before I completed the writing, I made sure that the final, finished *picture of the completed book* was on the wall in front of me. I showed copies of it to certain friends of mine, and I faxed it to others, as I worked to make the dream a reality.

Why did I do all that? I knew it would literally help me create the end result. It did.

I have done that with every book I've ever written. I couldn't imagine writing a book without being able to see it—and its *results*—in advance.

Does the goal create the picture? Yes, it does.

161

Does the picture in your mind create the goal? Yes, it does.

THE FACTS ABOUT DREAMBUILDING

Look at these facts about what you now call "dream-building":

● The greatest achievers, in every civilization we have known, were considered to be "dreamers" during their lifetimes.

● Early creative thinkers drew their ideas on paper before they created them. Not having photographs, they drew their ideas on parchment and paper, so they could study them.

● Scientists now know that the more you focus on any picture or subject, the stronger you will chemically, physically, "imprint" that picture in your brain.

● Present-day neuroscientists have discovered that the process of "visualizing" is an actual, chemical process that creates physical thought "pathways in the brain."
They've discovered that the more you think about, or "visualize" any picture, the stronger neural "highways" you'll build about that picture.
The thought, the picture, or the dream, repeated often enough, creates actual chemical "pathways"—neural highways that your brain is designed to follow.

162

In short, dreambuilding actually imprints pictures of your future so strongly, that the brain actively works to make those pictures *happen*. You give your brain the plan to follow, and it follows that plan.

WHAT HAPPENS TO YOU NEXT
IS *NOT* AN ACCIDENT

That means what happens to you next is no accident. The brain is designed to follow the mental pictures you focus on *most*. It's like making Xerox copies of a picture over and over again, sending them to your computer-like brain, and saying, "Here are your instructions. Make it happen."

Every time you do that, your brain is making a print of whatever you're running through the copy machine. The more you reprint the same picture, the more times you are telling your brain: *"Make a copy of this. Print it. Make it permanent."*

The troubling thing is that the part of the brain you send all your Xerox pictures to, doesn't know which of them are true or false, or right or wrong, or something to avoid, or a goal you want to set. To the brain, to your own internal goal-seeking mechanism, all of the pictures you feed it are treated just the same: INPUT.

DREAMBUILDING IS A WAY TO CONTROL
WHAT YOU *THINK*

Real dreambuilding is learning to control your INPUT.

What kinds of pictures do you give to your computer control center—your own brain—in the average day?

What do you do in an average day? How much daily news do you watch? How does your average day at work go?

Do you argue at home, or do you get along? How much time do you spend being angry? What opinions do you have? How do you express them?

Are you in control of what you think, and what you say, or do you simply react to the daily demands, the opinions, the news briefs, and the popular attitudes of the world around you?

Do you set aside time every day to think about who you are, where you are, what you really want to achieve, and where you're going—or do you get up, go to work, come home tired, eat dinner, watch TV, go to sleep, and just get up again the next morning?

What if, just to dreambuild for a moment, you decided one day to put yourself completely in control of your own life—of all the "input" that you got—of your own "dreambuilding," not just now and then, but every moment. Every minute.

"DREAMBUILDING" ISN'T SOMETHING YOU DO *NOW AND THEN*—DREAMBUILDING IS A *WAY OF LIFE*

Real dreambuilding is not a now-and-then thing. It's an *attitude*. It's a *belief* you have about yourself that *no one* can shake.

164

Dreambuilding isn't only how you feel when you look at the car—or the home of your future; dreambuilding is how you look at *yourself.* Right now. Every moment. Every day.

Who are you—really? What do you *really* want?

If you had to take the "test" right now, and you had to answer what you would *really* want to do with your life, if you could—what would you say?

Dreambuilding isn't just about what you can buy. *Your* dreambuilding, the building of *your* dreams, is all about *how much you are willing to believe you are worth.*

IF YOU CAN'T *BELIEVE*, HOW CAN YOU *DREAM*? AND IF YOU DON'T HAVE THE *DREAM*, HOW CAN YOU *BELIEVE*?

How can you even begin to dream if you don't believe in your dream in the first place?

Or, if you aren't the kind of person who *believes* in dreams, how can you even *think* about making some "impossible" dream come true?

The answer may surprise you: When you first have the dream, *you don't have to believe in dreams to make them come true.* You just have to be willing to keep feeding the messages to your brain long enough for it to kick in, take action, and go to work on the problem.

The part of your brain that processes your messages, like your own Self-Talk, is designed to print every message you give it, *whether you believe in the message or not.*

To your brain, dreams are really nothing more than pictures of you in some future situation, played in advance.

Since the brain is designed, like a computer, to act on the strongest programs you give it, whatever future pictures you give it most, that's what it'll work hardest to accomplish. Like the computer, your brain has no choice.

It *has* to act on the strongest programs you give it. It was *designed* to.

THE MORE BELIEF YOU CREATE, THE BETTER IT WORKS

On the other hand, if you *do* believe in your dreams, the brain will work even harder to make those dreams come true. Why? Because belief creates strong emotions. And emotions are actually chemical stimulators in the brain that make the brain work harder; it's like giving an engine higher octane fuel.

Some of the strongest mental programs you have right now are programs you got that had strong emotions attached to them. So those particular programs are chemically stronger. You can test this out for yourself. For a moment, stop and think about something that happened to *you* in your childhood that *you'll never forget*. Get a good picture of it in your mind.

Whatever you just thought of, there are emotions attached to that picture—that program—in your brain. Maybe you got punished for something, or maybe it was something positive like getting a special reward, or perhaps it was moving to a different home, or your first bicycle, or visiting someone far away, or maybe a very memorable birthday party. Those kinds of pictures tend to be strong because when they happened to us, our emotions were strong, we pumped more chemicals into those programs in the brain—and so they remain strong, unforgettable to this day.

Imagine putting that level of feeling, intensity, sincerity, determination, enthusiasm, into the messages and pictures you see of your future.

The more you make yourself believe in those dreams, the more energy you'll give them, and the stronger they'll be. The stronger they are, the harder your brain will work on them *all on its own*!

HOW CAN DREAMBUILDING HELP YOUR BUSINESS?

How can this skill of dreambuilding help your business now—and give new life to the rest of your life?

It can help you in three important ways:

A. When you visualize your future, in a positive way, you create positive program pathways in your brain. It's like giving a computer good instructions instead of bad instructions. Dreambuilding gives your personal "mental" computer some of the best instructions you can give yourself.

B. Dreambuilding makes you *think*, and makes you

167

choose. It makes you consider what you have, what you don't have, and what you would *like* to have in your life. Thinking about that is healthy. And a sufficient amount of thinking about your station in life often prods you into taking action—doing something about it.

C. Dreambuilding makes you set goals. Good goals. Prosperous goals. Goals that you set and reach by your own hard work. Setting good goals—and writing them down on paper—is the first action step to creating success in anything you'll ever do.

Dreambuilding builds the desire that creates the goal.

WHAT TO DO:

1. Build your future every chance you get. Dreambuild. Get the picture of you being successful as a way of life. Imagine it, visualize it, focus on it, and make it the best picture of you and your life that could possibly be imagined. Then go to work on it.

2. Always follow up dreambuilding with writing down goals. Talk about your dreams. Write them down. The more you do this, the greater chance you'll have of achieving each of them.

3. Always take dreambuilding seriously. Never make fun of yourself (or anyone else) for reaching beyond the ordinary. Go ahead . . . dream! But always take it seriously.

168

I have great respect for the old saying which says, "Be careful of what you want . . . you'll probably get it." My experience has been that that may be one of the most accurate truths of life.

If that is true—that what you dream about, or think about most, is what you *will* end up with—then it makes great sense to dream great dreams. If you're going to *get* what you dream about most, then you should dream the *best* for yourself.

Why not? The dreams you're willing to think about create an important part of your thoughts. Your thoughts create your actions. Your actions create the results: Small dreams lead to small results. Great dreams lead to great results.

THE RIGHT SELF-TALK
WILL HELP YOU REACH YOUR DREAM

Your own Self-Talk can set your dreams in the right direction, by helping you build the right positive mental programs that will get you where you want to go.

In the next chapter, we'll look at some specific Self-Talk that will help you make those dreams a reality—as well as giving you some other positive programs along the way.

Meanwhile, go ahead. *Dream.* And when you dream, make it good; that's where you're taking the rest of your life.

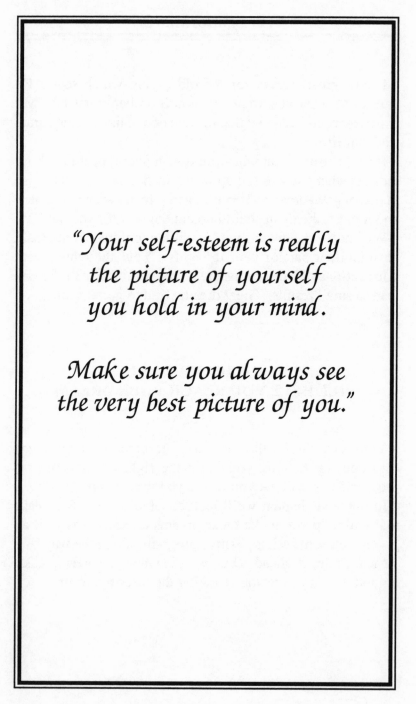

"Your self-esteem is really
the picture of yourself
you hold in your mind.

Make sure you always see
the very best picture of you."

Chapter Thirteen
A New Set Of Self-Talk Scripts
For Amway

hen I wrote the book *"Network Of Champions,"* I wrote a special set of Self-Talk scripts for Amway Distributors, and included them in the book.

Almost as soon as distributors started reading the book, I began to get requests for additional Self-Talk scripts. The request was, in each case, that once again the additional scripts would be written *specifically* for Amway Distributors.

After reviewing your requests carefully, I decided to write several new Self-Talk scripts that I believe will give you some immediate help. I've included those scripts for you here.

Because this isn't a book about Self-Talk, the following brief explanation will help those newer distributors who may not have heard of Self-Talk or understand anything about it.

Self-Talk is the name we use for the process of creating positive new programs in the brain.

Like a computer, the brain is designed to get programmed. From the moment we're born we start to get "messages" from the world around us; first our family, then friends and school, television, and everything that happens around us.

HOW WE GET OUR SELF-ESTEEM

What the scientists learned next is especially important to you, if you'd like to have some control over your own future, and if you'd like to have the kind of self-esteem that works *for* you instead of holding you back.

They didn't know until recently that every message you ever receive—every "input" you get—from anywhere and everywhere—is *programmed* into your brain, much like anything you type into a computer. And those programs you've been getting are actually recorded in something like chemical "highways" or pathways in the brain.

All those programs, those mental messages we get, form the basis of our self-esteem—what we believe most about ourselves.

Everything you think about, everything you do, or say, in every area of your life, is based on the strongest "pathways" that have been recorded in your brain.

YOUR OWN SELF-ESTEEM AND SELF-BELIEF ARE AT THE HEART OF BEING A SUCCESS IN THE BUSINESS

Your self-esteem, then, is a result of the programs you got while you were growing up—and are getting even now. Low self-esteem creates low self-belief.

That's why the person with low self-esteem never achieves any great success in life.

That's why some people believe they don't have a chance. That's why some people have no self-confidence, or any sense of quality and importance about their lives at all. They got the wrong programs.

That's also why some people do better in the business than others. It's not luck.

Fortunately, scientists have learned you can *change* old programs with the right kind of Self-Talk. This isn't some kind of "new age" concept, or some occult theory (all of which I'm soundly against). Self-Talk is based on years of solid medical research. It's practical, it works, and anyone can use it.

IF YOU'D LIKE TO CHANGE, YOU *CAN*

If you get new programs that are really strong, and if you get those new programs repeated over and over, the old physical pathways will lose their strength.

They become something like old unused highways that are broken down and filled with cracks and weeds. Like those old highways we would never want to drive on, the brain follows the newest, neatest, strongest, biggest, fastest, pathways it can.

And Self-Talk is the best way we've found so far to build

173

those new highways in the brain.

But *this* time, we're not letting negative friends, or uninformed teachers at school, or the bad news on the six o'clock news do our programming *for* us. *This* time, with the help of clear, accurate, *correct* programming messages— that's Self-Talk—*this* time we choose to get it right.

(For a more detailed explanation of how Self-Talk works, refer to *"Network of Champions."*)

And a final note: Self-Talk scripts are always worded in the "present tense," as though what you're hearing about yourself has *already* taken place. That's because what you're really doing is giving very specific directions to your *computer*— your brain, telling it how you want it to be, and what you want it to do.

Even with the most positive-sounding Self-Talk, you're not trying to kid yourself. You're just giving your own mind a *completed blueprint* instead of a *sketch* or a *suggestion*.

People who don't understand Self-Talk say, "I plan to take my business seriously." Experienced Self-Talkers know to say, *"I take my business seriously."* Before you know it, they do.

THE AMWAY SCRIPTS

During the past fifteen years I've written and recorded specific Self-Talk scripts in many of the key areas of personal growth. Those scripts, like basic language tapes, teach people the basic "language" of Self-Talk.

During that time literally millions of people have learned how to use Self-Talk. That includes medical doctors, teachers, students, motivational authorities, business people—and especially Amway Distributors who want to do everything they can to build a successful business.

Initially all of the Self-Talk scripts were "general." That is, none of them were written specifically for Amway Distributors. But now, here is the *second* set of Self-Talk scripts written especially for you. To avoid confusion with the six scripts I included in *"Network of Champions,"* which were numbered #1 through #6, I've numbered these six *new* Amway scripts, Self-Talk scripts #7 through #12.

After these six new scripts, you'll find some helpful tips on how to put them into practice in your business.

A SPECIAL SCRIPT FOR PROSPECTING

This first script needs no explanation. It's one of the most requested Self-Talk scripts and tapes ever.

SPECIAL AMWAY DISTRIBUTOR
SELF-TALK SCRIPT #7

"SELF-TALK FOR PROSPECTING"

I choose to be good at prospecting—and I am.

The telephone is my friend. And so are the people I talk to on the phone.

I never put off making a prospecting call. I pick up the phone and I make the call.

Every time I talk on the telephone, I smile. It changes the sound of the words I say.

When I prospect in person, I'm always confident and professional.

I'm building my business, so I do what it takes. I make my list, I make my contacts, and I show the plan.

I have confidence. I like what I'm doing, and it shows. And I prospect every chance I get.

I believe that everyone I meet, find, or who comes into my life, could do even better by being in the business. So I invite them in.

I am never too shy or embarrassed to speak up, introduce myself, and set a time to show the plan.

Every time I think about prospecting, I think about being my best.

I choose to be very good at prospecting, and I choose to be very good at building my business.

I'm building a business that's mine. I'm building a future that works.

I'm good at prospecting. I choose to like it, I choose to be good at it, and I choose to make prospecting a positive part of my life.

When it comes to building my business, nothing stops me or gets in my way. I create my success. And I prospect every day.

I prospect. I show the plan. I build my business.

I have a great opportunity to share with the world. When I'm prospecting, I'm letting them know I have something to share with everyone I meet.

Every time I see the stars in the nighttime sky, I think about two things. First, I think about how many people there are who are waiting to see the plan. And then I think about being a Diamond.

I choose to succeed. I believe in the business, and I believe in myself. I prospect. I show the plan. And I reach my goals.

That is the kind of Self-Talk that can help you turn every prospect into a potential friend, and make the process easier. The more you focus on positive Self-Talk for prospecting, the easier it will be—and the faster your business will grow.

AMMUNITION FOR YOUR ATTITUDE

One of the biggest problems you face when building your Amway business is the problem of *negativity*—in others and even sometimes in yourself.

Almost all of our reaction to negativity is unnecessary. And yet the problem is so important I devoted a whole chapter to it in this book. Whatever kind of negativity you have to deal with, the following Self-Talk can work wonders.

SPECIAL AMWAY DISTRIBUTOR
SELF-TALK SCRIPT #8

"SELF-TALK FOR OVERCOMING NEGATIVITY"

I have a good attitude, and it shows.

I'm positive about my business, and positive about myself.

I never allow negativity of any kind to choose my attitude for me.

I make the choice to be optimistic, positive, confident, and in control.

I refuse to let negatives into my life. I listen only to people who believe in the best.

178

I am one of the most positive, upbeat, optimistic people I know. I set an example for everyone around me.

When I feel down, I get myself up. I have the choice, each day, and each moment, to be in charge of how I feel. And I choose to feel great!

I have an incredible attitude. To me, life is a blessing, and I can't wait to live it.

I never let negative people get me down. I keep myself up. That's my choice, and I live it every day.

Any time someone says or does anything that could spoil my day, I take charge of my attitude, think good thoughts, and get on with my day. And it works!

I may not be able to change the people around me, but I can always change myself. And I make sure I'm always at my best.

I'm up. I'm positive. I feel good about myself. Life is good! I have a goal, and I'm making it work.

No one has the right to darken my day. So I don't let them. I always see the bright, sunny, positive side of life.

Negativity never stands in my way. Anytime I run into a negative thought, I erase it, and I replace it.

I choose to believe in the good things in life. I'm busy building my business and making my life work. I only have time to be positive.

That's the kind of Self-Talk that can turn your day around—and keep your business on the right track.

BUILDING YOUR SELF-ESTEEM

Making a success of your Amway business builds a lot of self-esteem. But what can you do when you're not quite there yet? You work at building your self-esteem along the way, with every forward step you take.

Read the following Self-Talk script every day for a week or two, or listen to the Self-Talk Cassette of this script every night just before you say your prayers and go to sleep. You'll wake up differently in the morning.

SPECIAL AMWAY DISTRIBUTOR
SELF-TALK SCRIPT #9

"SELF-TALK FOR BUILDING STRONGER SELF-ESTEEM"

I know that my self-esteem is really the picture I hold of myself in my mind. So I make sure that I always see the very best picture of me.

I'm good to myself. I take care of myself, I believe in myself, and I improve myself in every way I can.

I build self-esteem by believing in my future, reaching my goals, and making my business work.

I help other people improve their lives. And when I do, I improve my own self-esteem.

I have a positive, healthy opinion of myself. I work hard to be a person of quality in every way.

I never leave my own self-esteem up to anyone else. I'm responsible for feeling good about myself.

I know that I alone am responsible for building my character, choosing my values, creating my attitude, and making my life work.

Every night, before I go to sleep, I think about the good I've done that day.

I care about the people who matter in my life. And now I've learned to care about me too.

I respect others and I respect myself. I trust others and I trust myself. I like other people and I like myself. What I hope to find in others, I make sure I create in myself.

I'm one of my own best friends. I like how I think. I like what I do. Because I care about myself, I have a friend for life.

181

I never take my self-esteem for granted. I work at it, I build it, and I take full responsibility for me.

I like who I am; I'm happy with me. I build myself up, and I set myself free.

People like me. They respect me and they appreciate me in many positive ways. I choose to be well-liked and respected.

Other people notice that I am a person of quality and character. That's because I choose to live my life that way.

Everything I do with my life is my choice. So I choose to like myself, build myself up, care about myself, and make my life work.

Self-Talk for building self-esteem is one of the most popular subject areas of all, perhaps because it personally applies to *everyone*.

I want to make it clear, though, that the kind of self-esteem building we're talking about here is not in any way designed to conflict with your spiritual beliefs, or create a wrongful sense of pride. In fact, the *opposite* is true: Self-Talk is specifically designed to help you make the most of the God-given mechanism called the human brain, and to encourage you take personal responsibility for making the *most* of the life you have been given.

A NEW PARTNER IN YOUR BUSINESS

You may be surprised at how much more you can get out of the tools you're using right now. Are you alert, aware, on top of every detail? Is your business IQ working at its best? Are you the sharpest you've ever been?

Use the following Self-Talk for a few weeks and you'll make "tools" your new partner in your business. And that's a combination that works!

SPECIAL AMWAY DISTRIBUTOR
SELF-TALK SCRIPT #10

"SELF-TALK FOR USING THE TOOLS"

I choose to improve my life in every way I can. When I think of the future, I think of the word "Success."

I use the tools. Tools are the keys that open the doorways to my success.

I learn something new every day. I will not let a day go by without getting better.

I listen, I learn, I reinforce, and I remember.

I never put off using the tools. I make sure I've got the tools I need, and I make sure I use them.

When I wake up in the morning and before I go to sleep at

183

night, I always read a book, listen to a tape, or use a tool that will help me grow.

When I use the tools, I keep myself informed, motivated, educated, edified, and more determined to succeed than ever.

I know that using the tools every day helps me make my business grow. So I make sure I use the tools every day.

When it comes to improving my life, I know that tools are not an option—tools are essential. I use the tools, and I build my business.

When I use the tools, I prepare myself for success.

I choose to make my business tools a positive investment in building my life and my future.

I know that the more I use my business tools, the greater the chance for my success. I use the tools, and I make my business work.

I have made the decision to learn everything I can about my business, and to practice what I've learned.

I know that I am responsible for using the tools, motivating myself, showing the plan, and making my business succeed.

I always find the time it takes to use the tools each day. And I like the way I learn new things easily and naturally.

184

I have made the decision to make my Amway business my career. I choose to succeed. So I use the tools.

BUILDING A BUSINESS THAT WORKS

This next script is one you can refer to often, or one Self-Talk tape you may want to play a lot. If there's one thing you could do to help your future, it would be to build your business. If there's one thing you could do to build your business, it would be to make the following Self-Talk an everyday part of your life.

SPECIAL AMWAY DISTRIBUTOR
SELF-TALK SCRIPT #11

"SELF-TALK FOR BUILDING MY AMWAY BUSINESS"

I build my Amway business every day. And every day, my business gets better.

When I build my business, I build my future. When I build my business, I create my success.

I take my Amway business seriously . . . very seriously. This is my career. This is my life.

I take responsibility for building my Amway business. No

185

one has to motivate me to work the plan and make it work. I am responsible for my success.

I believe in this business. I know it's right, and I know it works. And I know the rest is up to me.

I prospect, I show the plan, I use the tools, I invest the time, I learn from my upline, I build my downline, and I succeed.

I don't see building my business as taking my time—I see building my business as doing the most important thing I've ever done.

My dream is to make my business work. I build my business every day, and I make my dreams come true.

This is for my family. This is for my freedom. This is for my future. And this is for my dream.

I'm a leader. I'm moving forward. I've made the commitment to succeed, and I'm making my business work.

My Amway business gives me the opportunity to succeed in every important area of my life. This business builds my faith, my family, my friendships, my freedom, and my future.

The Amway business is awesome, amazing, fantastic, incredible, unbelievable, and unstoppable. And not only that, it's real.

I'm a nonstop, do-it-now, make-it-happen, get-it-done, go-for-it achiever—and I'm going all the way!

I'm listening! I'm learning! I'm motivated! I'm fired up! And I'm making it happen!

I choose to work for myself. I choose to become financially independent. I choose to have freedom for the rest of my life, and I choose to succeed. I choose Amway.

I have made the decision to build my Amway business—and I build it EVERY day!

With Self-Talk like *that* on the team, you can't *help* but do what you know it takes to build your business! When you build the programs that support *that* kind of attitude, your business will grow—because you're taking control of doing what you need to do, when you need to do it.

A SCRIPT OF SELF-TALK
DESIGNED ESPECIALLY FOR *YOU*

I know the first time you read this next Self-Talk script, you may think it doesn't apply to you. But I'd like you to reconsider. What if it *does*?

If you plan on using Self-Talk on a regular daily basis, and especially if you listen to Self-Talk Cassettes, I encourage you to read or listen to this next Self-Talk, even if you think it's not about you! If you think it's not about you, you should make it a *point* to use this particular Self-Talk often.

Here's why. When we first hear Self-Talk that sounds too good, we try to reject it. We automatically think things like, "That's not me," or "I could never do that," or "Yeah . . . sure!" in the most disbelieving kind of way.

But remember, that's just proof that your old programs don't have a picture of you being that terrific or that successful. That's exactly what you have to defeat if you want to have real happiness and freedom in your life.

FOR NOW, GO AHEAD AND BELIEVE

When you read this next Self-Talk script, I'd like to ask you to do something special, both for you and for me. I'd like to ask you to read this script, and just for now, put your disbelief aside.

Instead of saying, "That's not me," I'd like you to tell yourself, "That *is* me!"

We all know anyone can pretend. So even if you tend to be the skeptical, disbelieving type, for the next minute or two, *pretend*. Imagine. Visualize. *Believe*. Even if just for now. Later, when you're rereading this script or listening to it on tape, you can do the same thing again. You can *believe*.

There's one thing you can be sure of. If you made this one script a part of your life, every day, day after day, for, say, the next two or three months, you would probably become the person this script is talking about.

Care to try it and find out? What do you have to lose? After all, what *else* were you planning to do with the next five, or ten, or fifteen years of your life?

So here goes.

You get to pretend. You get to put all your disbelief under your chair and imagine you're sitting on a throne of your own, in your castle . . . your incredible, amazing, new home—and all of your most unbelievable dreams are coming true . . . because . . . you actually *are* . . . a *Diamond*.

SPECIAL AMWAY DISTRIBUTOR
SELF-TALK SCRIPT #12

"SELF-TALK FOR
GOING DIAMOND"

I am a Diamond. I may not be there yet, but I will be, because inside of me, I am a Diamond.

I have what it takes. I can go all the way to the top. I have made the choice to go Diamond.

I choose to be a Diamond. I choose to succeed in my life in every way.

I have decided to believe in myself. I'm going Diamond, and there is nothing that can stand in my way.

I have vision. I know how to dream. I see myself living that life, walking across that stage, feeling great, and knowing that I did it.

I like having freedom in my life. I like being successful in every way. I like reaching every goal I set. And I really like going Diamond.

Going Diamond is real. It works. Going Diamond is not only possible, it is something I can do.

I have set the date to go Diamond. I have the goal, the plan, and I know the date I'm going to make it.

I've decided not to wait, and not to put it off. I can do this. I'm going Diamond starting now.

I am a Diamond. I'm a Diamond in my heart, in my mind, in my plan, and in my actions.

Diamonds are people who are special. I am someone who is special. That means I can be a Diamond.

I choose to be a Diamond. In my mind, every day, I'm already there. And every day, I work hard to become the Diamond I know I am.

I know that the freedom I create, is the freedom I deserve. I know that the success I choose, is the success I achieve.

This is the message I want myself to hear: I'm building my business. I'm going Diamond.

Can I do it? Yes I can! Can I be a Diamond? I already am! I'm going Diamond!

I'd suggest you put those words to work for you. If any of those Self-Talk scripts apply to you or your business, it's time for you to take the next step—it's time to put them into practice.

WHAT TO DO:

1. Read one or more of the scripts to yourself at least once each day. Self-Talk is best used first thing in the morning, and just before you go to sleep at night. (You can use Self-Talk during the day, too—and if you're using tapes, an especially good time to listen is while you're driving in the car.)

2. Make photocopies of the scripts and put them in your planner where you'll see them often. Just before you pick up the telephone, if you find yourself hesitating, reread one of the scripts.

3. Listen to Self-Talk on tape. Years of research have proven that the best way to learn Self-Talk, and the easiest and most effective way to change your old programs, is by listening to Self-Talk tapes.

All of the Self-Talk scripts you see in this book have been professionally recorded on cassettes in an album called "*The Victory Tapes.*" I recommend that you get the prerecorded Self-Talk Cassette versions of those scripts and play them often. (The cassette publisher's name and address are included in the back of the book for your convenience.)

THE MOST IMPORTANT THING YOU CAN DO

I've never been one to recommend anything unless I believe in it strongly myself. Self-Talk is a good example of something I believe in. If you want to really make your business happen, you should get Self-Talk tapes and you should use them. They'll help you build your business.

Tapes of that type give you immediate help *while* you're changing your programs, because they boost your attitude and put you in motion *now*, while you're listening.

Instead of trying to record your own voice on a tape recorder at home, I suggest that you use the professionally-recorded tapes. Listening to Self-Talk in your own voice usually works against you. (When you hear yourself, you're hearing your own worst critic talking to you.)

The single most important thing I can recommend for you to do in order to move your business forward is *to change the old mental programs that have been holding you back.*

Just imagine what you could do for your business in a single week—or month, or year—if the old programs were no longer in control of *you*, because they had been *replaced* with the right kind of positive *new* programs!

If the new programs seem strange to you at first, don't worry about it. Just keep building the new highways that will take you where you want to go.

Program in the new truths about you—and you'll make them come true.

Now let's take a look at another way to build your belief—and your business.

"The Amway business
is awesome, amazing, fantastic,
incredible, unbelievable,
and unstoppable.

And not only that,
it's _real_."

Chapter Fourteen

One Hundred Reasons To *Be* In The Business, And *Stay* In The Business

I recently completed a smaller, gift-size book entitled, *"100 Reasons To Be In The Business And Stay In The Business."* In that book I identified and listed one hundred of the most important benefits people receive from building their Amway businesses.

I then defined each of the benefits, using examples that had come from my several years of research into the Amway business.

The entire contents of that book would be too lengthy to reprint here (it fills over a hundred pages), but I thought it would be helpful to give you the list of the hundred reasons by themselves, even if I didn't have room here to include the explanations and the examples that go along with each reason.

If you're already a distributor, I recommend you keep this list handy so you can read it again anytime you want to re-arm yourself with the facts.

If you're not yet in the business, the following few pages

will acquaint you with the real truth about the people and the benefits of the Amway business.

As you read these pages, I encourage you to put aside any preconceptions or misconceptions you might have had about what it really means to be "in Amway." What follows is the result of an extensive, objective study into what this business is really about.

As you read the list, ask yourself if any other company, any other business, any other career path *anywhere* could list the potential benefits that this list represents. Nothing else I've ever discovered comes even close. This list, when taken in its entirety, is logical, accurate, and almost overwhelming. It is *very* convincing.

TEN IMPORTANT AREAS OF YOUR LIFE
THAT YOUR AMWAY BUSINESS CAN CHANGE

I've divided the list into ten categories representing several of the main areas of your life. The list isn't intended to be in any specific order. Something that may be the most important reason to you may have a different importance to someone else.

At first glance, some of the reasons on the list might sound similar, but if you think them through, you'll see they're not the same. "Owning your own business" is not the same thing as "Being your own boss." "Setting goals," as an example, is different than "Knowing where you want to go," even though they are both great benefits of being in the business.

A GREAT CHECKLIST FOR SETTING
YOUR GOALS

If you choose, you can make a copy of the entire list and put it into your planner where it will always be handy.

The list is also designed to be used as a checklist; it's a great tool to have when you're setting goals! As you read through each of the benefits on the list, put a check mark in the boxes next to each item that's important to you.

The list can also be used when you're discussing the business with prospects. When you ask people which of the following benefits *they'd* like to have, I think you'll find that the 100 Reasons is a "want list" of benefits almost *anyone* would like to have.

What great motivation it is to see the real facts of the Amway business all lined up where you can't miss them! Here they are.

100 REASONS TO *BE* IN THE BUSINESS
AND *STAY* IN THE BUSINESS

Your Family Life

☐ 1. Give your family an environment of success.
☐ 2. Be in a business that focuses on your family.
☐ 3. Send your kids to the schools and colleges of your choice.

196

☐ 4. Teach your own children good work habits.

☐ 5. Spend time with your kids.

☐ 6. Build your business with your children, and for your children.

☐ 7. Spend your time working with your mate.

☐ 8. Teach your family the value of goals, work, and independence.

☐ 9. Give your children the great parenting opportunity to watch you work.

☐ 10. Be the best parent you can possibly be.

Your Career

☐ 11. Be in the #1 business of its kind—anywhere.

☐ 12. Work at something that works—long term.

☐ 13. Be your own boss, and be in charge of your career.

☐ 14. Choose where you want to work.

☐ 15. Set your own hours.

☐ 16. Do something truly valuable with your time.

☐ 17. Work with people who are willing to help you succeed.

☐ 18. Follow a value-based business plan that has proven success.

☐ 19. Spend your time working at something you like.

☐ 20. Be in a business that is *the future*.

Your Personal Growth

☐ 21. Get out of any rut you might be in.

☐ 22. Learn the great rewards of patience and delayed gratification.

☐ 23. Learn how to dream—and learn how to make the dream come true.

☐ 24. Add to your education.

☐ 25. Become a more positive person.

☐ 26. Build your self-esteem.

☐ 27. Build more self-confidence.

☐ 28. Become comfortable in front of others.

☐ 29. Get rid of your imagined limitations.

☐ 30. Be more motivated, and have more enthusiasm.

Your Financial Future

☐ 31. Begin building long-term financial security.

☐ 32. Have more discretionary income.

☐ 33. Get rid of money worries.

☐ 34. Have more than you need.

☐ 35. Always be able to pay the bills on time.

☐ 36. Always have money in your pocket or purse.

☐ 37. Be able to make investments.

☐ 38. Own your own home.

☐ 39. Get out of debt.

☐ 40. Earn the money it takes to have freedom in your life.

Improving Your Success

☐ 41. Never again waste your time going nowhere.

☐ 42. Be able to have the things you've dreamed of having.

☐ 43. Show yourself—and the world—you were right.

☐ 44. Always be able to dress well, and feel good about yourself.

☐ 45. Choose where you want to live.

☐ 46. Have the home you want.

☐ 47. Go where you want to go.

☐ 48. Say "Yes" to opportunities instead of "No."

☐ 49. Do what you want to do, when you want to do it.

☐ 50. Create a success attitude that stays with you every day.

Reaching Your Personal and Professional Goals

☐ 51. Live in an environment of setting and reaching goals.

☐ 52. Learn the skills you need to reach your goals.

☐ 53. Measure your own progress—on a daily, weekly, monthly, and yearly basis.

☐ 54. Learn that you can reach any worthwhile goal you set.

☐ 55. Work on your goals with the people you care about most.

☐ 56. Always know exactly what you have to do to reach your goals.

☐ 57. Always have the tools you need to help you reach your goals.

☐ 58. Build a track record of reaching your goals, and a natural habit of being successful.

☐ 59. Live in a world where reaching goals is part of the plan.
☐ 60. Know exactly where you want to go.

The People You Spend Your Time With

☐ 61. Work with the people you want to be with.
☐ 62. Associate with people who share your beliefs and values.
☐ 63. Associate with people who are positive.
☐ 64. Be with others who encourage and motivate you.
☐ 65. Have people in your life you can look up to and respect.
☐ 66. Spend time with others who are also working to improve their lives.
☐ 67. Stop spending your time with negative people.
☐ 68. Surround yourself with successful people.
☐ 69. Build positive friendships that can last a lifetime.
☐ 70. Get to know a "family" of reliable people who believe in you.

Improving the Quality of Your Daily Life

☐ 71. Take time for yourself when you want to.
☐ 72. Be able to enjoy your life each day.
☐ 73. Be able to pursue positive interests.
☐ 74. Be able to relax.
☐ 75. Focus on your dreams, and be able to expect them to come true.

☐ 76. Have peace of mind.

☐ 77. Deal with problems in a more positive way.

☐ 78. Choose to be a success.

☐ 79. Do what makes your life work.

☐ 80. Get off the job/home/job merry-go-round.

Creating a Future that Works

☐ 81. Always be able to look forward to tomorrow with positive anticipation.

☐ 82. Know that you have an exciting future—and you get to build it for yourself.

☐ 83. Look forward to retirement—because it will mean something entirely new to you.

☐ 84. Plan on being right about building your future.

☐ 85. Be in a business that can help you improve in every area of your life.

☐ 86. Create new friendships that will add to your life.

☐ 87. Reach a higher level of positive expectancy and achievement in your life.

☐ 88. Watch your children grow, in the business.

☐ 89. Strengthen the most important relationships in your life (God, family, etc.).

☐ 90. Live up to your best—every day—in every way.

Making a Difference in the World Around You

☐ 91. Help others live up to their best.

☐ 92. Be able to support a cause or charity you believe in.

☐ 93. Teach others.

☐ 94. Do something important with your life.
☐ 95. Know that you count.
☐ 96. Be important to others.
☐ 97. Have a lifetime career and a lifestyle where you're always able to learn something new.
☐ 98. Be able to share your success with others.
☐ 99. Help other people find a whole new life.
☐ 100. Build a legacy that will live beyond you.

* * *

AND THAT'S JUST THE BEGINNING

There are more reasons, of course. The complete list of reasons I've compiled goes on a lot longer, but those I've included here get the point across.

You probably have reasons of your own. Put them all together, and it's clear that this business has a lot going for it. No other business has a list of benefits that reads like this one. That's because there *is* no other business like this one.

That list is more than just a list of reasons to be in the business. It's a summary of the attributes that make one person's life work better than another's.

These are the building blocks that form the foundation of a lifetime of success. When you bring these attributes together—in one remarkable business, you have *all* of the foundation blocks, not just a few of them.

When you have a business that brings it all together—*the values, the freedom, the people, the belief, the dream, and the future*—you have a remarkable business.

When you bring it all together, you have Amway.

"The success of your business will never be based on chance.

It will be based on learning everything you can, practicing everything you learn, and perfecting everything you practice."

Chapter Fifteen
Repeat, Practice, and Perfect

I f I could put everything I've written in this book into one simple, easy-to-read chapter, this would be it. Though I hope all the chapters in this book are to the point, and easy enough to read, this is the chapter where all the key points are brought home.

This is a review that is designed to be read in a few minutes—or studied carefully. It's also designed to be a checklist of important *action* steps you can take to improve your business.

I encourage you to read this chapter as often as possible, to *repeat, practice,* and *perfect.* There are some things you only learn when you read them more than once—when you repeat them.

Sometimes it takes repeated readings to get the message. Or, if it's a tape you're listening to, you have to listen to it more than once to get the full meaning of the message that's being communicated to you.

Some motivational authorities have said that we never

really understand any new concept completely until we've read or heard that concept explained, in the exact same words, at least eight times. Based on my own years of research on how the brain works, I believe that's true.

A QUICK REVIEW THAT WILL HELP YOUR BUSINESS EVERY DAY

It's been said that it isn't how *much* you read—it's what you *learn* from what you read that counts. I'd agree with that, but I'd add something to it: it isn't what you *learn*, it's what you *do* with what you learn that *really* counts.

What follows is a quick review that you can use and reuse often. To make the review information simple, I've arranged it into *Action Steps*, and I've also included *Key Points* for you to highlight and remember.

I suspect the more you read and review the Action Steps and Key Points that follow, the better—and faster—your business will grow.

REPEAT, PRACTICE, AND PERFECT

Action Step #1:
Learn everything you can at Amway Distributor University.

205

This really is an institute of higher learning. Take advantage of it. This is the real thing. Success 101. Learn from the Amway teachers at ADU for the next few years and you'll move right on past all those others who only *thought* they had an education that would prepare them for the 21st century.

KEY POINT: Even though Amway Distributor University doesn't have a campus with old brick buildings and graduation ceremonies with caps and gowns, ADU is one of the most important educational institutions operating today.

And regarding graduation ceremonies with caps and gowns, I've seen the typical kind, and I've seen the Amway kind. I'd take Emerald and Diamond ceremonies any day.

Action Step #2:
Learn the Six "Rules of Tools."

Take them from the book or type them out and post them on the wall of your Amway office. The "Six Rules of Tools" are:

1. If you want to succeed in the business, tools are not an option—they are essential.

2. Use the tools every day. Not now and then. *Every day*.

3. Tools aren't a negative *expense*; tools are a positive *investment*.

4. The more you use the tools, the greater your chance for success.

5. Treat tools with the greatest respect. Tools give you knowledge. *Knowledge is your future*.

6. Tools are the keys that open the doors to your future. Make sure you have all the keys you need.

KEY POINT: Watch out for the worst kind of poverty: the poverty of the *mind*. Impoverished minds seldom recognize their need to have the tools that will help them succeed. The more you bring the tools of teaching into your life, the stronger and more successful you will become.

Action Step #3:
Attend every Amway seminar and function.

Like using the tools, if you want to become successful, attend the seminars and functions.

KEY POINT: Seminars and functions in the Amway business may sound like, and *feel* like, inspirational pep rallies.

Never underestimate them. They may be motivational, and they may be inspirational. But in fact, they are key steps in your training in the business.

Here's what *really* happens when you attend:

1. You associate with anyone and everyone else who is in the same business as you are. (How much more open information and sharing can you get?)

2. You learn, first-hand, from the best of the best—from the men and women, real people, who have actually been there. Those teachers who talk to you from stage are usually Emeralds or Diamonds. Every one of them, at one time, has been exactly where you are now.

3. 90% of success in any business is *attitude*. You will never find a better attitude than the incredible attitude that

happens at an Amway function. If you want to find the good in life, the good that's really out there, *attend, attend, attend.*

If you want to be smart, and surround yourself with positive people—attend every Amway seminar, meeting, or function you have in front of you.

4. When you attend, you have the opportunity to reset your sights. Think about your goals. Ask yourself where you've been and what you've been doing. Get down to the basics of where you're going and what you're going to do next. Face up to the commitment all great people face when they decide to succeed.

Amway functions get you to do that. If you did nothing more in your Amway business than to do that—this business would be incredibly important to you, just for that insight alone.

However, being in the business, and going to the functions, does more than that. In every essential way, attending the meetings and functions shows you the importance of the business you're in.

Action Step #4:
Never, ever, again, let the fear of prospecting stand in the way of your success.

I've worked in the field of human behavior long enough to know that just saying, *"there's nothing to be afraid of,"* doesn't make you feel the slightest bit better, even for a moment, if someone wants you to openly prospect the next three people you meet. Or the next . . . *one* person you meet.

But let me tell you a true story that could help you the next

208

time you think about prospecting.

BE CONFIDENT, BE YOURSELF, AND SAY WHAT YOU HAVE TO SAY

We've been told that the greatest single fear almost any person can face is the fear of having to stand up in front of a crowd of people and speak.

I know that's true, but I also speak to a lot of audiences. All of them are Amway audiences, and most of them are very large, sometimes tens of thousands of people in an audience.

So here's what I do. Before I walk up on that stage, with all the lights, and all the music, and all the crowd before me, I do two things:

The first thing I always do, without fail, is to spend a few minutes backstage with my wife Elise, in a very private, quiet moment of prayer. We always pray that I'll say it well. And most important, we both pray that what I tell you will go home with you, and that it will help.

The second thing I do before I go on stage is to get a clear picture of *you* in my mind. And then I imagine something extraordinary. I imagine that not only are you the most important person in my life, a family member or a close friend, but I also imagine that this one time is the last time I will ever be able to talk to you.

And then I think, if you were members of my own family, or if you were my closest friends, what would I say to you if this were the last chance I would ever have to say anything to you at all?

209

How can you be afraid, if you really care about the people you're talking to?

Prospecting is probably easier for most people than speaking in front of twenty or thirty thousand people on a stage. But the answer to getting over the fear, in either case, is to just *be yourself.* Care about the people you're talking to. Be honest. Have courage. And say what you have to say.

Action Step #5:
Get past the Four Fears of Prospecting:

1.   Defeat the *fear of rejection* by constantly letting yourself know that the prospect is your *friend.*

Try this for yourself. You might be surprised at the results you get. Many of your prospects *will* become your friends when they enter the business and join your team.

KEY POINT: If it bothers you to be told "No," there are two things you should do that can help. The first is to build your own attitude—before you make the contact and after. You can choose to accept the "No" in a negative way, or you can go right past it, look forward, and don't slow down.

Next, work on your prospecting skills. You may need to get some help on this one. If you're qualifying your prospects properly, and saying exactly the right thing, your percentages should climb. Meanwhile, keep using the right Self-Talk.

2. Defeat the *fear of the unknown* by putting one foot in front of the other and always taking the next step.

Go ahead and take the risk—take the next step—even if the

fear is there.

We tend to be too afraid of being afraid. Go ahead. Be afraid. It really doesn't hurt you, because what you're fearing is all imaginary anyway.

Meanwhile, because you're willing to take the risk and make the contact in spite of your fear, you become more familiar both with your prospect and the skill of prospecting. The result is that you're no longer dealing with an unknown.

3. Defeat the fear of failure by never again basing your belief in yourself on the limited beliefs of others.

Set your own standards—and don't worry what the rest of the world thinks. I know we were all raised to worry about what other people think. But now is a good time to change that.

When you set your own standards, the whole idea of "failure" becomes unnecessary. Maybe you don't reach some particular goal the first time you try to reach it, but that doesn't mean *failure*—it means you learned something, and you're still alive and going for it! That's all it means. You didn't hit the mark, so you try again. You keep doing it. You get it right.

KEY POINT: Keep the word "success" in your vocabulary. Get rid of the word "failure." And don't worry what other people think.

4. Defeat the *fear of work* by always remembering that when you're building your Amway business, *work* really means *freedom*.

KEY POINT: Change the meaning of the word "work."

211

Instead of seeing your work in the business as a "job," always see your work as "*freedom*."

Action Step #6:
Rate your skill at showing the plan by completing the self-test in Chapter Eight.

Review your skills now, and then mark your calendar to review yourself again six months from now. Use the review as a checklist for those skills you need to work on most.

KEY POINT: Make a photocopy of the checklist, check off the areas you're going to work on, and put it in plain sight on the bulletin board in your Amway business office. Just before you show the plan, run through the checklist. It'll keep you on your toes, and your presentation will get better.

Action Step #7:
To improve your presentation, put your belief in gear.

Your prospect will always know if you believe in the business. The more you believe in it, the more it will show.

KEY POINT: Before every presentation you make, build your belief. Listen to a tool tape, listen to Self-Talk, reread your goals, and make certain you believe in yourself and you believe in the business.

Action Step #8:
To improve your presentation, make your Amway business your most important business.

Your prospect will know if you're taking the business seriously. It will show in everything you do and say. You don't even have to be at a higher level in the business, and already successful, to prove that this business is your life. But you do have to *make* it important for your business to *be* important.

Action Step #9:
To improve your presentation, always, always, always be a *professional*.

Review the professional skills checklist in Chapter Nine. Instead of overlooking or going past any of the points because you think they don't apply to you, assume that *all* of the points apply to you. They do.

KEY POINT: Being a professional—all the time—doesn't mean you have to wear designer clothes and speak with a Harvard accent. It means you work at perfecting every professional skill you can—and practice them every chance you get.

KEY POINT: Have someone take a photograph and make a cassette recording of you showing the plan now. Then take another photograph and make another cassette recording of you showing the plan three months from now.

I've been learning how to present ideas to people for more than thirty years. I still frequently record my presentations and study them. I use video and I use audio cassettes. I also debrief after every presentation I make. That is, I go over my presentation to find ways I could have communicated the information better.

You should do the same, every time you show the plan. You can always get better. You can always improve. But you have to take it seriously, listen carefully, be objective, not feel criticized, and constantly work to get better. That's what professionals do. That's how professionals *live*.

Action Step #10:
Never, ever listen to the negative opinions of others.

There are two kinds of people in the world: those who listen to other people's negative opinions—and those who don't. This rule of success is very simple. *Never, ever live your life based on the negative opinions of others.*

Most of them are either wrong, uninformed, or they don't know what they're talking about in the first place.

KEY POINT: Never let negative people rob you of your belief, your spirit, your enthusiasm, your energy, or your dedication. They have none of these. Why should they take yours from you?

Action Step #11:
Decide to be a pro at dealing with negative people.

Start by learning to identify the two types of negative people:

1. People who are negative or critical because they are *un*informed or *mis*informed.

These are people who aren't always negative. But they may be being critical only because they don't know anything about the business, or because they got the wrong information about the business.

KEY POINT: These are people who need information. They're not trying to discourage you—they just don't know the facts. Don't let their momentary negative attitude get to you. Learn to react to these people by giving them the facts.

2. People who are negative *as a way of life*.

These are people who are generally negative about everything. You can see it in such telltale signs as the way they look, how seldom they smile, how many *other* things in their life they're negative about, how critical they are, and how they listen—or *refuse* to listen—to new ideas.

KEY POINT: Once you've pegged a negative person as someone who is negative as a way of life, move on. Unless you're married to that person, there's little you can do to change him. Or her.

KEY POINT: If the truly negative person is either yourself or someone you care about and perhaps even live with, you can help.

Negative people were programmed to be that way, usually when they were young. To overcome the old programming you have to constantly feed and nurture that person—even

215

yourself—with new, positive, healthy programs.

As you build positive self-esteem, the older, negative programs will be replaced by the new programs of self-acceptance, self-worth, and a more positive self-image.

It takes time and effort to do this, but if you love the person, or if it's you, and you want to care about yourself, changing a negative into a positive is worth all the effort you put into it.

Action Step #12:
Turn off the television. Really. No kidding. This one is very serious. Turn it off.

There's just no excuse to waste three, or two, or even *one* hour a day getting your mind programmed for failure by what most people watch on TV. If you want to get your life in order, turn off your television for one month, and ask yourself how you feel.

KEY POINT: This one is hard for most people to actually put into practice. Even the idea itself sounds radical (which should tell you how important your television time really is).

The reason it's hard to put into practice is because people don't take the problem seriously.

Take it seriously. The single most important brick wall that stands between you today, working for a living, and you becoming financially independent, and a Diamond in the business a few years from now, is probably your television set. *Turn it off.* Your life will change.

Action Step #13:
Make dreambuilding a part of your everyday life. Not just now and then—all the time, every day.

Dreambuilding is a *skill*. You have to learn how to do it. You have to practice doing it. And if you want to succeed, you have to get good at it.

Once you learn it, practice it, and get good at it, the skill of dreambuilding will literally change your life. Here's what to do:

1. Build your future by seeing it in advance, every chance you get.

2. Always follow up dreambuilding with writing down goals.

3. Always take dreambuilding seriously.

KEY POINT: A lot of distributors seem to think that dreambuilding is something you do at functions, or now and then as a motivational exercise.

Wrong. Do it all the time. Every day. *Always* see yourself as how *you choose* to be. Make dreambuilding something you practice so often you do it without having to think about it.

KEY POINT: Before you can live the dream, you have to be able to see it in your mind.

Action Step #14:
Use and practice the right kind of Self-Talk, every day, every chance you get.

217

I've worked in the field of personal motivation for most of my adult life. In all that time, and with all the research, I've never found any one idea that is more effective for changing old negative programs in the brain, than using Self-Talk in the right way.

What you say, what you think, and what you do, each moment, every day, is the result of the strongest programs that are imprinted in actual chemically-recorded pathways in your brain.

Exactly like the programs that are typed into your own personal computer, the strongest programs that have been typed into your brain are the programs, or pathways, you automatically follow.

If you've got the right programs already, your life is probably working well. If you have programs that are negative, or working against you, those are usually the same programs that are keeping you from doing what you need to do to be a success in the business.

KEY POINT: Self-Talk is a practical way of changing old negative programs in the brain and replacing them with healthier, positive new programs that create successful attitudes and actions.

KEY POINT: The best way to learn Self-Talk, and change old programs, is by listening to Self-Talk Cassettes. Listening to Self-Talk tapes, played quietly in the background, has the same result as typing new programs into your "mental computer."

People who listen to Self-Talk usually experience better

attitudes, an increase in physical energy and enthusiasm, a greater sense of focus on goals, and greatly-increased self-esteem.

KEY POINT: Listening to specially-worded Self-Talk scripts on cassettes should never take the place of listening to the "tool" tapes available to you through your upline. The right Self-Talk always helps you get *more* from every business tool you use.

Action Step #15:
Read the special Self-Talk scripts for Amway Distributors in Chapter Thirteen, or listen to those specific scripts on Self-Talk Cassettes.

The Self-Talk Scripts that are included in Chapter Thirteen were written specifically to deal with some of the most important problems and opportunities you deal with as an Amway Distributor.

If you aren't familiar with the effects of using this kind of Self-Talk, my suggestion is that you take it seriously and give it a try.

1. Read one or more of the scripts to yourself at least once each day.
2. Make photocopies of the scripts and put them in your planner where you'll see them every day.
3. Listen to Self-Talk on tape.

KEY POINT: There are many Emeralds and Diamonds today who will tell you that it was Self-Talk of this kind that helped them get where they are today. They worked the plan like everyone else has to, of course, but many of them will tell you that it was the new Self-Talk that made the difference.

KEY POINT: Never underestimate the importance of using Self-Talk to give you the right kind of "success programs." Not only will listening to Self-Talk change your old programs, it will motivate you, and keep you on track while you're reaching your goal.

Action Step #16:
Use the "100 Reasons To Be In The Business . . ." when you're prospecting, showing the plan, or motivating yourself.

I mentioned in an earlier chapter that I recently wrote a special, "gift-sized" book called *"100 Reasons To Be In The Business And Stay In The Business."* It wasn't intended to be a book—I just started listing the reasons why you ought to be in the business—and stay in the business, and I then wrote solid supporting information for each of the reasons I had compiled.

When I got done, I had written what is probably the most logical—and the most compelling—argument for being in the Amway business I've ever read, or heard, anywhere.

I wasn't able to print it all here, but I *was* able to give you the "short version"—the 100 Reasons, even if they didn't include the persuasive commentary I wrote for each of the 100 Reasons in the original book.

But even without the rest of that book to back you up, I

220

wanted you to have, in *this* book, at a minimum, the list itself.

So I included the "100 Reasons" in this book to help you with your business right now.

KEY POINT: If you ever wonder whether or not you should make your Amway business your prime professional focus in life, set aside five minutes from your busy life, and read the list. Read it out loud. Discuss it with your spouse and your family. You'll know what to do next.

The list I've included in Chapter Fourteen is, without a doubt, the most incredible list of reasons to be in a business I've ever seen.

And just as important, there is no other business of any kind, anywhere, that could copy that list—and call it their own.

There are other reasons to build your Amway business, of course. I'm sure you have your own. Add your own reasons to the list.

If ever you're ever in doubt about the business, reread the list. Discuss it with your wife, or your husband, or your partner in the business. It will help remind you why you're in the business in the first place.

KEY POINT: You can use the list of 100 Reasons as a prospecting tool.

I've thought of a number of ways you can use the list of 100 Reasons when you're prospecting or showing the plan. You'll probably think of other ways to use it on your own. Use the list of 100 Reasons however you choose. But by all means, *use it.*

USE THIS REVIEW CHAPTER TO *REPEAT*, *PRACTICE*, AND *PERFECT*

Take the opportunity to *repeat*, *practice*, and *perfect*, when it comes to getting good at what we've discussed in the pages of this book.

This review chapter should give you the basics, and make it easy for you to reinforce the key points you'd like to use when you're building your business.

I know that if you take what you've read so far, and apply it directly to your Amway business, your business will grow.

And that is, after all, what this business is all about. Growing. Getting better. Rising above yourself, and reaching a whole lot more of the potential you were born with.

That's the kind of knowledge that's worth *repeating* in your own life, day after day, every way you can.

That's the kind of ideas that are worth *practicing*.

And that's the kind of business that is worth *perfecting*.

"Every time you see the stars
in the nighttime sky,
think about two things.

First, think about
how many people there are
who are waiting
to see the plan.

Then think about
being a Diamond."

Chapter Sixteen

The Dream Is Real—The Time Is Now

hat did you have in mind to do with the rest of your life? If you haven't already made plans to do something special, I hope you'll reconsider.

Do you have any idea how capable you really are? Do you really understand what you could do with the rest of your life if you really wanted to? Has anyone ever sat you down and told you how *good* you are, what you *can* do, what you *can* achieve?

Because of Amway, you now have something in common with every other person everywhere, who wants to make his or her life work—doctors, teachers, housewives, steel workers, waiters and waitresses, neurosurgeons, business managers, college students, engineers, salesmen and women—whoever you are, wherever you are. From the moment you are shown the plan, you have the same unlimited opportunity as everyone else.

So if you want to do something special with your life,

perhaps, more than anything else, it gets back to that one word: *belief.* Belief in the *business* and belief in *yourself.*

If you could look into the future and see yourself being incredibly successful, being free, then maybe it would be easier for you to make the commitment *now* to make your dream come true.

But in a way, you *can* look into the future. If you decide to make this business work, you can predict your own success.

The truth cannot be denied; it's been done before. Again, and again, and again. And as I pointed out earlier, the commitment to building the Amway business not only works, it has become predictable—generation after generation.

MAKE THE COMMITMENT—TO THE *BUSINESS* AND TO YOUR OWN *FUTURE*

I began this book with the story of the Victor family, and three incredible generations of success. I've met many of them, and gotten to know them. I'm quite certain if you were to talk to any of them, and asked them if they thought *you* could do what *they* did, the very first thing they'd say would be that there isn't the slightest doubt that you can do it if you commit to doing it.

The first generation of Amway Distributors had nothing to go on but the dream—and their faith. But they also made the commitment, and in the process, they made history.

Then the second generation came along. They had seen the business work for their own parents, and they *knew* they could make it work for themselves, too.

And then the third generation arrived, and they, too, knew they would succeed if they made the commitment for themselves.

Joe and Helyne Victor saw the dream, had the belief, made the commitment, and never gave up. The only thing they had to guide them was what they held in their hearts.

Jody Victor, second generation Direct, who with his wife Kathy is now a revered Crown in the business, didn't only follow in his father's footsteps—he followed the plan. He and Kathy made the commitment, and made it work.

Steve Victor became the first, third generation Direct in the business. And something special happened when he and his wife Marcia crossed the stage to be recognized as new Direct Distributors: they proved the dream, and once again proved one of the principles on which the business was founded: *there are no limits.* It is a business without end.

THE BEST IS YET TO COME

When Joe Victor stood on that same stage, together with his own son and grandson, all living proof that *the dream is real*, Joe Victor said something that showed the heart of someone who knows how to dream.

"We feel so fortunate," he said, "to be here, and around this long, and see all the things that have happened, and all the people whose lives have been changed for the better. And we know what a tremendous future they have, and *you* have."

And then he continued, with a great salute to the future of

the business, by adding, *"If I had one wish, I think I'd want to be one of the grandsons!"*

He sees the future . . . and you're in it!

Jody Victor, renowned for his leadership and his undying belief in the principles on which the business was founded, was talking about *you* when he said, "I know there will be many people who will come behind us. And they'll take it to even greater heights. And if we've done our job right, if we stick to our principles, and if we stick to the things that made this business so endearing to thousands and hundreds of thousands and millions of people . . . it's going to be a phenomenal road ahead."

You can trust these people. I know I do. They have been there. Just like your upline and your leaders in the business—they've all been there, and they know: *This is just the beginning.*

Jody and Kathy Victor spend all their time building the future—and sharing it with others. As Jody said, "Who knows how big it can be? *How big can you dream?*"

YOUR OWN PERSONAL VICTORY

I sincerely hope that in the pages of this book you have found some of the recognition you deserve, some tools and ideas you can put into practice, some motivation to help you stay with it, and some inspiration to make the commitment to make your future work.

Perhaps the best summary of my feelings about the opportunity in front of you are in the words of a letter I wrote to all of the distributors in your organization, and published in the USA Today newspaper in the United States. That letter was entitled, "An American Victory." In that letter I said:

"After a long and careful evaluation of who you are, what you do, and why you are successful, there are some things you should know about YOU, as an Amway Distributor.

"First off, you made a good choice! You are a member of one of the finest, most positive, and worthwhile organizations in the world today. You represent free enterprise at its greatest, and personal growth at its best.

"You are not only building a business, you are creating a better life—for yourself, for your family, and for the rest of the world around you.

"You have the right tools, the right plan, and the right attitude. If you are presently an independent Amway Distributor, you are in the right place. *Stay with it.* If you have not yet become a part of this exceptional group of people, you should.

"Whether you are just getting started, or you are experienced in the business, one thing is clear: *the best is yet to come.*"

**NOW IS THE TIME. THIS IS THE PLACE.
YOU ARE THE ONE.**

It has been several years now since I first began to find members of your organizations, sitting in the audience when

I was giving talks and seminars about success. I've gotten to know a lot of you during that time.

When I first met many of you, you were just starting out in the business. Now, just a few years later, many of you are Emeralds and Diamonds. We meet again, year after year, when I come to speak at your Dream Nights and Reunions and Free Enterprise Days.

And each time I meet you, though I'm thrilled at your success, I'm not surprised. You made a commitment. And you're in the business.

What impresses me so much about you, however, is that when I first met many of you, you were just getting started—just seeing the dream. And now, the dream has become real, life is working, and you've found the freedom you were looking for.

You were good people, working a job, not always sure where you were going, until one day, someone showed you the plan.

To all of you I've met along the way, who are now reaching your goals in the business, *congratulations!* I knew you could do it. I'll look forward to seeing you again, and shaking your hand, as you reach even greater heights on your pathway to your dreams.

And to all of you who are just getting started, or are just now making that commitment to reach *your* dreams, I'll look forward to meeting you, too, as you build your business and make your own dreams come true. I believe in you. I know you can do it.

I hope by now I've made it clear how important I believe you are. Yours truly *is* an American Victory.

God bless you, and keep doing it!

Dr. Helmstetter can be reached at:
Amvox (regular line) 798-7101
Amvox (Diamond line) 459-2975

For information on currently available Self-Talk Cassettes, including a special set of Self-Talk Cassettes for Amway Distributors, featuring the Self-Talk scripts which are included in this book, you may contact the publisher of Self-Talk Cassettes directly at 1-800-982-8196.

*To order additional copies of the book **"American Victory,"** or to order "Network Of Champions" or "One Hundred Reasons To Be In The Business And Stay In The Business," contact your upline, or call 1-800-982-8196.*